SPECTRUM

An Anthology of Short Stories

Edited by

JAYA SASIKUMAR
PAUL GUNASHEKAR

Orient Longman

Contents

Acknowledgements

For permission to use copyright material the publishers are grateful to the following:

Kewlian Sio and Writers' Workshop, Calcutta, for 'Let's Go Home' from *Its a Small World and Other Stories* by Kewlian Sio; Ernest Hemingway and Charles Scriber's Sons, New York, for 'A Day's Wait' by Ernest Hemingway from *American Literature—An Anthology and Critical Survey;* Chinua Achebe and Heinemann Ltd., London, for 'Marriage is a Private Affair' from *Girls at War* by Chinua Achebe; K. A. Abbas and Kutab Popular Limited, New Delhi, for 'Sparrows' from *Rice and Other Stories* by K. A. Abbas; Progress Publishers, Moscow, for 'Mother of a Traitor' by Maxim Gorky from *M. Gorky: Selected Short Stories*; William Heinemann Ltd., London, for 'The Verger' by Somerset Maugham from *The Complete Short Stories of Somerset Maugham: II*; Oxford University Press for 'Kong Yiji' by Lu Xun (tr. Gladys Yang) from *Modern Chinese Short Stories* ed. W. J. F. Jenner; Alan Sillitoe and W. H. Allen Ltd., for 'On Saturday Afternoon' from *Saturday Afternoon* by Alan Sillitoe.

Introduction

In selecting the twelve short stories for this book we had in mind a student who needs an introduction to the study of literature as a step towards a more formal study of the subject at the university. The two main tasks that we therefore set ourselves were: (*a*) that the stories should provide a wide spectrum of the best that is available in the field, and (*b*) that the selections made should be so used that they give the learner a foretaste of some of the essential tasks that belong to a study of literary works of distinction.

To meet the first requirement we have included stories from eight different lands and four different continents. There are stories from three English-speaking countries—Britain, the United States and Canada, stories from India, China and Nigeria, and a story each from the U.S.S.R. and France. In thus spreading our net so wide we have worked for one other distinctive feature for this anthology—to make it represent a variety of themes as well as a variety of styles of writing.

Our second task—of making this selection serviceable to beginners in literary studies—called for a special set of exercises which should help the learner in specific ways to enter the world of literary works. To realise this objective we have had to extend the scope of the book's editorial apparatus. Like many such anthologies this one too provides introductory notes, contextualised glosses for new words and phrases, and comprehension questions (both global and local) in order to facilitate the reader's understanding of the subject matter. But unlike most such anthologies it goes beyond the usual type of exercise to train its reader's critical faculty. It does so through a section called 'Steps to Interpretation' which leads the learner towards a critical understanding and appreciation of the distinctive features of each story—its theme, its quality and character and its style of presentation.

Editors

Fur

Saki

Hector Hugh Munro (1870–1916) the Scotsman who wrote under the pen-name of Saki was a talented writer of wit and vivacity. After his mother's death when Munro was only two, his father (who was a police officer in Burma) sent him to England to be brought up by his aunts. Finishing his studies, Munro served in the Burma police. This was only for a short while. He returned to England to become a newspaper correspondent—and journalist. He soon became well-known as a satirist and his political sketches (*Alice in Westminster*) were published in 1902. But it is as a master of short stories that Munro is remembered. His collections of short stories are *Reginald* (1904), *Reginald in Russia* (1910), *Beasts and Super-Beasts* and *When William Came* (both 1915). During World War I, he enlisted in the army and was killed in action.

Most of Munro's stories are delightfully light-hearted with a sting of satire hidden somewhere in them. In *Fur*, two young women plot together to make a wealthy old man buy an expensive present for one of them.

'You look worried, dear,' said Eleanor.

'I am worried,' admitted Suzanne; 'not worried exactly, but anxious. You see, my birthday happens next week—'

'You lucky person,' interrupted Eleanor; 'my birthday doesn't come till the end of March.'

'Well, old Bertram Kneyght is over in England just now from the Argentine. He's a kind of distant cousin of my mother's, and so enormously rich that we've never let the relationship drop out of sight. Even if we don't see him or hear from him for years he is always Cousin Bertram when he does turn up. I can't say he's ever been of much solid use to us, but yesterday the subject of my birthday cropped up, and he asked me to let him know what I wanted for a present.'

'Now I understand the anxiety,' observed Eleanor.

'As a rule when one is confronted with a problem like that,' said Suzanne, 'all one's ideas vanish; one doesn't seem to have a desire in the world. Now it so happens that I have been very keen on a little Dresden figure that I saw somewhere in Kensington; about thirty-six shillings, quite beyond my means. I was very nearly describing the figure, and giving Bertram the address of the shop. And then it suddenly struck me that thirty-six shillings was such a ridiculously inadequate sum for a man of his immense wealth to spend on a birthday present. He could give thirty-six pounds as easily as you or I could buy a bunch of violets. I don't want to be greedy, of course, but I don't like being wasteful.'

'The question is,' said Eleanor, 'what are his ideas as to present-giving? Some of the wealthiest people have curiously cramped views on that subject. When people grow gradually rich their requirements and standard of living expand in proportion, while their present-giving instincts often remain in the undeveloped condition of their earlier days. Something showy and not-too-expensive in a shop is their only conception of the ideal gift. That is why even quite good shops have their counters and windows crowded with things worth about four shillings that look as if they might be worth seven-and-six, and are priced at ten shillings and labelled "seasonable gifts".'

'I know,' said Suzanne; 'that is why it is so risky to be

vague when one is giving indications of one's wants. Now if I say to him: "I am going out to Davos this winter, so anything in the travelling line would be acceptable," he might give me a dressing-bag with gold-mounted fittings, but, on the other hand, he might give me, Baedeker's *Switzerland*, or *Ski-ing without Tears*, or something of that sort.'

'He would be more likely to say: "She'll be going to lots of dances, a fan will be sure to be useful".'

'Yes, and I've got tons of fans, so you see where the danger and anxiety lies. Now if there is one thing more than another that I really urgently want it is furs. I simply haven't any. I'm told that Davos is full of Russians, and they are sure to wear the most lovely sables and things. To be among people who are smothered in furs when one hasn't any oneself makes one want to break most of the Commandments.'

'If it's furs that you're out for,' said Eleanor, 'you will have to superintend the choice of them in person. You can't be sure that your cousin knows the difference between silver-fox and ordinary squirrel.'

'There are some heavenly silver-fox stoles at Goliath and Mastodon's,' said Suzanne, with a sigh; 'if I could only inveigle Bertram into their building and take him for a stroll through the fur department!'

'He lives somewhere near there, doesn't he?' said Eleanor. 'Do you know what his habits are? Does he take a walk at any particular time of day?'

'He usually walks down to his club about three o'clock, if it's a fine day. That takes him right past Goliath and Mastodon's.'

'Let us two meet him accidentally at the street corner tomorrow,' said Eleanor; 'we can walk a little way with him, and with luck we ought to be able to side-track him into the shop. You can say you want to get a hair-net or something. When we're safely there I can say: "I wish you'd tell me what you want for your birthday." Then you'll have everything ready to hand—the rich cousin, the fur department, and the topic of birthday presents.'

'It's a great idea,' said Suzanne; 'you really are a brick. Come round tomorrow at twenty to three; don't be late, we must carry out our ambush to the minute.'

At a few minutes to three the next afternoon the fur-trappers walked warily towards the selected corner. In the near distance rose the colossal pile of Messrs Goliath and Mastodon's famed establishment. The afternoon was brilliantly fine, exactly the sort of weather to tempt a gentleman of advancing years into the discreet exercise of a leisurely walk.

'I say, dear, I wish you'd do something for me this evening,' said Eleanor to her companion; 'just drop in after dinner on some pretext or other, and stay on to make a fourth at bridge with Adela and the aunts. Otherwise I shall have to play, and Harry Scarisbrook is going to come in unexpectedly about nine-fifteen, and I particularly wanted to be free to talk to him while the others are playing.'

'Sorry, my dear, no can do,' said Suzanne; 'ordinary bridge at threepence a hundred, with such dreadfully slow players as your aunts, bores me to tears. I nearly go to sleep over it.'

'But I most particularly want an opportunity to talk with Harry,' urged Eleanor, an angry glint coming into her eyes.

'Sorry, anything to oblige, but not that,' said Suzanne cheerfully; the sacrifices of friendship were beautiful in her eyes as long as she was not asked to make them.

Eleanor said nothing further on the subject, but the corners of her mouth rearranged themselves.

'There's our man!' exclaimed Suzanne suddenly; 'hurry!'

Mr. Bertram Kneyght greeted his cousin and her friend with genuine heartiness, and readily accepted their invitation to explore the crowded mart that stood temptingly at their elbow. The plate-glass doors swung open and the trio plunged bravely into the jostling throng of buyers and loiterers.

'Is it always as full as this?' asked Bertram of Eleanor.

'More or less, and autumn sales are on just now,' she replied.

Suzanne, in her anxiety to pilot her cousin to the desired haven of the fur department, was usually a few paces ahead of the others, coming back to them now and then if they lingered for a moment at some attractive counter, with the nervous solicitude of a parent rook encouraging its young one on their first flying expedition.

'It's Suzanne's birthday on Wednesday next,' confided Eleanor to Bertram Kneyght at a moment when Suzanne had left them unusually far behind; 'my birthday comes the day before, so we are both on the look-out for something to give each other.'

'Ah,' said Bertram. 'Now, perhaps you can advise me on that very point. I want to give Suzanne something, and I haven't the least idea what she wants.'

'She's rather a problem,' said Eleanor. 'She seems to have everything one can think of, lucky girl. A fan is always useful; she'll be going to a lot of dances at Davos this winter. Yes, I should think a fan would please her more than anything. After our birthdays are over we inspect each other's muster of presents, and I always feel dreadfully humble. She gets such nice things, and I never have anything worth showing. You see, none of my relations or any of the people who give me presents are at all well off, so I can't expect them to do anything more than just remember the day with some little trifle. Two years ago an uncle on my mother's side of the family, who had come into a small legacy, promised me a silver-fox stole for my birthday. I can't tell you how excited I was about it, how I pictured myself showing it off to all my friends and enemies. Then just at that moment his wife died, and, of course, poor man, he could not be expected to think of birthday presents at such a time. He has lived abroad ever since, and I never got my fur. Do you know, to this day I can scarcely look at a silver-fox pelt in a shop window or round any one's neck without feeling ready to burst into tears. I suppose if I hadn't had the prospect of getting one I shouldn't feel that way. Look, there is the fan counter, on your left; you can easily slip away in the crowd. Get her as nice a one as you can see—she is such a dear, dear girl.'

'Hullo, I thought I had lost you,' said Suzanne, making her way through an obstructive knot of shoppers. 'Where is Bertram?'

'I got separated from him long ago. I thought he was on ahead with you,' said Eleanor. 'We shall never find him in this crush.'

Which turned out to be a true prediction.

'All our trouble and forethought thrown away,' said Suzanne sulkily, when they had pushed their way fruitlessly through half a dozen departments.

'I can't think why you didn't grab him by the arm, said Eleanor; 'I would have if I'd known him longer, but I'd only just been introduced. It's nearly four now, we'd better have tea.'

Some days later Suzanne rang Eleanor up on the telephone.

'Thank you very much for the photograph frame. It

was just what I wanted. Very good of you. I say, do you know what that Kneyght person has given me? Just what you said he would—a wretched fan. What? Oh, yes, quite a good enough fan in its way, but still. . .'

'You must come and see what he's given me,' came in Eleanor's voice over the 'phone.

'You! Why should he give you anything?'

'Your cousin appears to be one of those rare people of wealth who take a pleasure in giving good presents,' came the reply.

'I wondered why he was so anxious to know where she lived,' snapped Suzanne to herself as she rang off.

A cloud has arisen between the friendships of the two young women; as far as Eleanor is concerned the cloud has a silver-fox lining.

New Words

cramped:	narrow
conception:	idea
sable:	beautiful dark fur
Commandments:	the ten laws given by God to Moses
stole:	woman's wrap worn over the shoulders
inveigle:	trick somebody into a place
side-track:	turn a person from his purpose
brick:	(colloquial) generous, kind-hearted person
ambush:	lying in wait to make a suprise attack
bridge:	card game for four players
solicitude:	concern; anxiety
muster:	collection
pelt:	animal's skin with the fur on it

Comprehension

1. What is Suzanne worried about?

2. When does Eleanor's birthday come? What does she tell Bertram later? Which one is true? Why do you think so?
3. Why can't Suzanne ask Bertram to buy her the Dresden figure?
4. Why, according to Eleanor, do shops have their counters and windows crammed with cheap things?
5. Why doesn't Suzanne want fans? What does she madly want? Why? Where is she going in winter? What does she get at the end?
6. What is Eleanor's plan to side-track Bertram into the shop where furs are sold? Does it work? Does it work in the way Suzanne wants it to?
7. How does Eleanor want her friend to help her? Does Suzanne oblige? What is her excuse? How does this affect her? Does Suzanne notice the angry glint in Eleanor's eye?
8. Why does Suzanne walk a few paces ahead of the others? How does Eleanor use this chance? How does she introduce the subject of *her* birthday?
9. What 'sob-story' does Eleanor tell Bertram? Do you think the story is real? Why?
10. What does Eleanor present Suzanne with on her birthday? What does the 'Kneyght person' give her. What does he give Eleanor?

Steps to Interpretation

1. The two friends in this story are a study in contrast. How are Suzanne and Eleanor different from each other?
2. 'Even quite good shops have their counters and windows crowded with things worth about four shillings, that look as if they might be worth seven-and-six, and are priced at ten shillings and labelled "seasonable gifts".' Can you spot similar flashes of humour in other parts of the story?
3. 'A cloud has arisen between the friendships of the two young women; as far as Eleanor is concerned the

cloud has a silver-fox lining.' Can you explain the humour in these lines?

4. What picture of old Bertram Kneyght do you get from the story?
5. Bertram Kneyght is only 'a kind of distant cousin' of Suzanne's mother. But why don't they let the relationship drop out of sight? What trait of human character is held up to ridicule here? Do you find more instances of the same kind in the story?

Let's Go Home

Kewlian Sio

Kewlian Sio (1936. . . . .) is a noted writer among the younger generation of Indo-Anglian writers. Born in Calcutta, and educated in Darjeeling, Sio now works for an advertising agency in Bombay. His collection of short stories *A Small World* (1960) was published by Writers' Workshop, Calcutta.
Let's Go Home is a brief but touching story of a child's grief.

It started when they were going to school in the school-bus. Someone started to talk about marbles, and he was always so interested in marbles that, as he listened, he began to forget. At first only a little, but as the fervour of the discussion increased, he joined in the talk and it was then that he forgot completely. And afterwards, he did not know how he could have forgotten like that. But perhaps it was not so strange after all. Everyone had always said he was 'too sensitive' and 'so absent-minded at this age'. Perhaps it was he who was strange.

The bus rolled in through the gates and crunched on the gravel. It was always the familiar crunch that told him they were in. They broke up and jumped out with their bags and boxes, and outside, as he stood waiting for the rest to come down, the morning hill air felt good and smelt cool, clean and fresh, and the birds were chirping in the row of trees that ran along the gravel way. When the last boy was out, the bus rolled out of the gates again and they crunched along the gravel towards the stone entry porch.

As they went in someone observed, 'Why, today's

Saturday! Always like Saturday because the next day is Sunday. Don't you?' He answered, 'Yes!'. He thought, Saturday; no day like it. Even class on Saturday was not as bad as on other days, and everyone, including the teacher, seemed happier with the prospect of the evening and the morrow.

For him, it was mainly the evening and fun at home with his mother—he had lost his father. On other days there was always homework to do and dinner to prepare. But on Saturday they both were free; he did only a little of the homework; and his mother finished cooking early. Saturday evening meant a lot to him. And then there was, of course, the matinee on Sunday, about the only excitement of a rather quiet day.

They passed the dining room. The boarders were still at breakfast and they could hear the boys talking and the clatter of plates and knives, forks, spoons, cups and saucers. There was such a noise. 'They're having plantains this morning,' Peter said, creeping up to one of the entrances. 'Hey, Whisky! Let's have a plantain,' he called out to the boy sitting at the table nearest to him. 'Whisky' scowled, but on second thoughts threw him a skin. It looked so funny that all laughed.

Class began at half-past eight. And since it was Saturday, it began with Reading, and Miss Moss reminded the boys of three coloured action postcards on her desk that went every Saturday to the first three boys who read best. It was an exciting period, always looked forward to. After Reading, came Arithmetic which did not fare well with him; he was always falling asleep and then having to write fifty lines. Today, Miss Moss did not assign him a task and only asked someone to rouse him; but he wondered why. Then they had English and that wound up Saturday morning.

He had lunch with the boarders and a few other day-scholars, and Mr. White, the master-in-charge, who had his lunch at another table with Mr. Brown and Mr. Black, gave him a helping of the teachers' pudding. He was such a sensitive boy; so that should have made him remember but since the marbles in the bus he had completely forgotten and was so happy.

In the afternoon they had History and Geography and, because it was Saturday, they went upstairs to the library for the last hour. There he read a tale about how a clever young prince foiled an evil ogre and escaped from its clutches. It was exciting and at the same time comical and he enjoyed it. He would tell it to his mother when he got home; she would like it, and he could enjoy it all over again with her. Then the bell rang: time to go home. Books were hurriedly put back and boxes were snatched up from the rear of the room where they had been left, and, except for the boarders waiting rather forlornly at their desks, everyone else dashed out as if home were a train they would miss if they were late.

He did not take a bus with the rest of the day-scholars this time, he walked it with four others: Ned, Ram, Peter and Gopal. As they walked along the road, with the green and daisy-covered hill on one side and the railed off-slope on the other, the sun was bright and warm and the sky was blue. They talked and laughed a lot. Today was Saturday and tomorrow Sunday. He picked up a blade of grass and nibbled at it while Ram slid his ruler along the railing. This evening, Ned was going to the pictures, Ram was going for ice-cream with his visiting uncle. Peter was going horse-riding. Gopal was going to a wedding. As for himself, he was happy, so happy. He would go home, and after a quick wash there would be lemon pie on the table, with a large slice ready on a plate for him. The thought made him want to hurry. His mother always made lemon pie on Saturdays. He would tell his mother the tale he had read at school, when they were at tea. And, after tea, they would go out into the garden. His mother would do some weeding. He would have to water his plants. Had he already watered them? He could not remember. He had better see about it, the first thing when he got home.

They had reached the short-cut to his home.

'Okay, see you Monday!' he said, ducking under the railing off the road, and picking his way down the slope. But just before he started he heard someone say, 'But he doesn't live. . .!' and then someone else saying 'Sh-sh-sh!' and then a lot of giggling. But he did not mind them, because as he picked his way down the short-cut his mind was so full and happy with the anticipation of home and his mother, of the lemon pie and the plants in the garden.

After a little while, he saw the red roof, bright in the sun, grinning wide and happy in the distance. He brightened and began running a little faster. In a little while more he would see the white sides of the house, the curtains flying in the windows and his mother waiting and waving from the kitchen.

But he had not gone very much further when, all of a sudden, clear out of the blue, there was something wrong; he could feel it. At first it was only a feeling, a suspicion; then it grew and thickened in him, it began whispering in his ear, 'Don't go!'. It swelled in him and became heavier and he had to slow down. He slowed down to a snail's pace and then came to a dead stop, thinking. Everything was so quiet and strange, a bird chirped in a tree and after the sound had died away, it seemed quieter and stranger.

He felt himself getting goose-pimples when he started to take a few steps further.

Then he saw that there were no flying curtains beckoning to him and all the windows were closed; the flowers and plants were drooping in a pathetic sort of way. And he had a sudden and full recollection: that he was not living there any more but up the hill at his aunt's, that the house was empty and his mother had died one week ago. At first, he just stood still, looking, not knowing what he should do. There was a big lump in his throat and he felt like crying. Then tears came into his eyes and he wanted to cry a lot. But he could only cry quietly.

New Words

ogre:	cruel man-eating giant (in fairy tales)
foil:	prevent somebody from carrying out his plans
forlorn:	unhappy, uncared for
giggle:	laugh in a silly way
beckon:	call
pathetic:	sad, pitiful.

Comprehension

1. '. . . . . .as he listened, he began to forget.' What did he begin to forget? At what stage in the story do you come to know of this?
2. Why did the boys (and their teacher) like Saturday? What was the main attraction for him?
3. How did he and his mother spend Sundays?
4. 'It looked so funny that all laughed.' What looked so funny? Would it have looked funny to an adult, one of their teachers, for example?
5. Miss Moss did not assign him a task for falling asleep that day; she only asked someone to rouse him. He wondered why. Can you imagine why?
6. What other little acts of sympathy did he receive that day? Did they make him remember it? Was he happy?

7. What did he decide to do when he read the story of the prince and the ogre? Why was he not able to do it?
8. What were his friends' plans for the evening? What was he going to do?
9. He heard someone say, 'But he doesn't live. . . . . Can you complete the sentence?
10. 'He had a sudden and full recollection.' What did the poor boy remember? Was his father alive? What had happened to his mother? When? Who was he living with?

Steps to Interpretation

1. Everyone had always said he was 'too sensitive' and 'so absent-minded at this age'. Do you agree? What instances of these traits do you find in the story?
2. 'Everyone dashed out as if home were a train they would miss if they were late.' This is a delightful piece of children's fantasy. Can you pick out any more from the story?
3. For a boy of his sensitivity, was absent-mindedness a blessing or a curse? Why do you think so?
4. The boy in the story is just referred to as 'he', no name is mentioned. Do you think this is deliberate? What effect does it have on the reader?
5. At the end of the story the boy suddenly realises he is all alone—his world shattered. The author describes his grief briefly. What effect does it have on you? Would you have liked the description to be longer and fuller? Why?

The Accursed House

Emile Gaboriau

Emile Gaboriau (1835–73) was a distinguished French writer of popular detective stories. He was one of the pioneers of this genre, and his works have been translated into many other European languages. In addition, he wrote several memorable stories in a light vein.

The Accursed House is one of his famous stories in which he presents a highly amusing situation. The Vicomte de B——, a rich landlord, generously decides to lower the rents of his apartments, but his tenants read in this gesture some sinister design and resolve to vacate their lodgings in a body. The story is thus a subtle satire on human nature.

The Vicomte de B——, an amiable and charming young man, was peacefully enjoying an income of 30,000 livres yearly, when, unfortunately for him, his uncle, a miser of the worst species, died, leaving him all his wealth, amounting to nearly two millions.

In running through the documents of succession, the Vicomte de B—— learned that he was the proprietor of a house in the Rue de la Victoire. He learned, also, that the unfurnished building, bought in 1849 for 300,000 francs, now brought in, clear of taxes, rentals amounting to 82,000 francs a year.

'Too much, too much, entirely,' thought the generous Vicomte, 'my uncle was too hard; to rent at this price is usury, one cannot deny it. When one bears a great name like mine, one should not lend himself to such plundering. I will begin tomorrow to lower my rents and my tenants will bless me.'

With this excellent purpose in view, the Vicomte de B—— sent immediately for the concierge of the building, who presented himself as promptly, with back bent like a bow.

'Bernard, my friend,' said the Vicomte, 'go at once from me and notify all your tenants that I lower their rents by one-third.'

That unheard-of word 'lower' fell like a brick on Bernard's head. But he quickly recovered himself; he had heard badly; he had not understood.

'Low-er the rents!' stammered he. 'Monsieur le Vicomte deigns to jest. Lower! Monsieur, of course means to raise the rents.'

'I was never more serious in my life, my friend,' the Vicomte returned; 'I said, and I repeat it, lower the rents.'

This time the concierge was surprised to the point of bewilderment—so thrown off his balance that he forgot himself and lost all restraint.

'Monsieur has not reflected,' persisted he. 'Monsieur will regret this evening. Lower the tenants' rents! Never was such a thing known, Monsieur! If the lodgers should learn of it, what would they think of Monsieur? What would people say in the neighbourhood? Truly—'

'Monsieur Bernard, my friend,' dryly interrupted the Vicomte, 'I prefer, when I give an order, to be obeyed without reply. You hear me—go!'

Staggering like a drunken man, Monsieur Bernard went out from the house of his proprietor.

All his ideas were upset, overthrown, confounded. Was he, or was he not, the plaything of a dream, a ridiculous nightmare? Was he himself Pierre Bernard, or Bernard somebody else?

'Lower his rents! Lower his rents!' repeated he. 'It is not to be believed! If indeed the lodgers had complained.' But they have not complained; on the contrary, all are good payers. Ah, if his uncle could only know this, he would rise from the tomb! His nephew has gone mad, 'tis certain! They should haul up this young man before a family council; he will finish badly! Who knows—after this—what he will do next? He lunched too well, perhaps, this morning.'

And the worthy Bernard was so pale with emotion when he re-entered his lodge, so pale and spent, that on seeing him enter, his wife and daughter Amanda exclaimed as with one voice 'why, what *is* it?'

'Nothing,' responded he, with altered voice, 'absolutely nothing.'

'You are deceiving me,' insisted Madame Bernard. 'You are concealing something from me; do not spare me; speak, I am strong—what did the new proprietor tell you? Does he think of turning us off?'

'If it were only that! But just think, he told me with his own lips, he told me to—ah! you will never believe me—'

'Oh, yes; only do go on.'

'You will have it, then!—Well, then, he told me, he ordered me to notify all the tenants that—he lowered their rents one-third! Did you hear what I said?—lower the rents of the tenants—'

But neither Madame nor Mademoiselle Bernard heard him out—they were twisting and doubling with convulsive laughter.

'Lower!' repeated they; 'ah! What a good joke, what a droll man! Lower the tenants' rents.'

But Bernard, losing his temper and insisting that he must be taken seriously in his own lodge, his wife lost her temper too, and a quarrel followed! Madame Bernard declaring that Monsieur Bernard had, beyond a doubt, taken his fantastic order from the bottom of a litre of wine in the restaurant at the corner.

But for Mademoiselle Amanda the couple would undoubtedly have come to blows, and finally Madame Bernard who did not wish to be thought demented, threw a shawl over her head and ran to the proprietor's house. Bernard had spoken truly; with her own two ears, ornamented with big, glided hoops, she heard the incredible word. Only, as she was a wise and prudent woman, she demanded 'a bit of writing' to put, as she said, 'her responsibility under cover'.

She, too, returned thunderstruck, and all the evening in the lodge, father, mother, and daughter deliberated.

Should they obey? Or should they warn some relative of this mad young man, whose common sense would oppose itself to such insanity?

They decided to obey.

Next morning, Bernard, buttoning himself into his best frock coat, made the rounds of the three-and-twenty lodges to announce his great news.

Ten minutes afterward the house in the Rue de la Victoire was in a state of commotion impossible to describe. People who, for forty years, had lived on the same floor, and never honoured each other with so much as a tip of the hat, now clustered together and chatted eagerly.

'Do you know, monsieur?'

'It is very extraordinary.'

'Simply unheard of!'

'The proprietor's lowered my rent!'

'One-third, is it not? Mine also.'

'Astounding! It must be a mistake!'

And despite the affirmations of the Bernard family, despite even the 'bit of writing' 'under cover,' there were found among the tenants doubting Thomases, who doubted still in the face of everything.

Three of them actually wrote to the proprietor to tell him what had passed, and to charitably warn him that his concierge had wholly lost his mind. The proprietor responded to these sceptics, confirming what Bernard had said. Doubt, therefore, was out of the question.

Then began reflections and commentaries.

'Why had the proprietor lowered his rents?'

'Yes, why?'

'What motives,' said they all, 'actuate this strange man? For certainly he must have grave reasons for a step like this! An intelligent man, a man of good sense, would never deprive himself of good fat revenues, well secured for the simple pleasure of depriving himself. One would not conduct himself thus without being forced, constrained by powerful or terrible circumstances.'

And each said to himself:

'There is something under all this!'

'But what?'

And from the first floor to the sixth they sought and conjectured and delved in their brains. Every lodger had the preoccupied air of a man that strives with all his wits to solve an impossible cipher, and everywhere there began to be a vague disquiet, as it happens when one finds himself in the presence of a sinister mystery.

Someone went so far as to hazard:

'This man must have committed a great and still hidden crime; remorse pushes him to philanthropy.'

'It was not a pleasant idea, either, the thought of living thus side by side with a rascal; no, by no means; he might be repentant, and all that, but suppose he yielded to temptation once more!'

'The house, perhaps, was badly built?' questioned another, anxiously.

'Hum-m, so-so!' No one could tell, but all knew one thing—it was very, very old.

'True! and it had been necessary to prop it when they dug the drain last year in the month of March.'

'Maybe it was the roof, then, and the house is top-heavy?' suggested a tenant on the fifth floor.

'Or perhaps,' said a lodger in the garret, 'there is a press for coining counterfeit money in the cellar; I have often heard at night a sound like the dull, muffled thud of a coin-stamper.'

The opinion of another was that Russian, may be Prussian, spies had gained a lodgment in the house, while the gentleman of the first storey was inclined to believe that the proprietor proposed to set fire to his house and furniture with the sole object of drawing great sums from the insurance companies.

Then began to happen, as they all declared, extraordinary and even frightful things. On the sixth and mansard floors it appeared that strange and absolutely inexplicable noises were heard. Then the nurse of the old lady on the fourth storey, going one night to steal wine from the cellar, encountered the ghost of the defunct proprietor—he even held in his hand a receipt for rent—by which she knew him!

And the refrain from loft to cellar was:

'There is something under all this!'

From disquietude it had come to fright; from fright it

quickly passed to terror. So that the gentleman of the first floor, who had valuables in his rooms, made up his mind to go, and sent in notice by his clerk.

Bernard went to inform the proprietor, who responded:

'All right, let the fool go!

But next day the chiropodist of the second floor, though he had naught to fear for his valuables, imitated the gentleman beneath him. Then the bachelors and the little households of the fifth storey quickly followed his example.

From that moment, it was general rout. By the end of the week, everybody had given notice. Everyone awaited some frightful catastrophe. They slept no more. They organised patrols. The terrified domestics swore that they too would quit the accursed house and remained temporarily only on tripled wages.

Bernard was no more than the ghost of himself; the fever of fear had worn him to a shadow.

'No,' repeated his wife mournfully at each fresh notification, 'no, it is not natural.'

Meanwhile three-and-twenty 'For Rent' placards swung against the facade of the house, drawing an occasional applicant for lodgings.

Bernard—never grumbling now—climbed the staircase and ushered the visitor from apartment to apartment.

'You can have your choice,' said he to the people that presented themselves, 'the house is entirely vacant; all the tenants have given notice as one man. They do not know why, exactly, but things have happened, oh! yes, things! a mystery such as was never before known—the proprietor has lowered his rents.'

And the would-be lodgers fled away affrighted.

The term ended, three-and-twenty vans carried away

the furniture of the three-and-twenty tenants. Everybody left. From top to bottom, from foundations to garret, the house lay empty of lodgers.

The rats themselves, finding nothing to live on, abandoned it also.

Only the concierge remained, grey-green with fear, in his lodge. Frightful visions haunted his sleep. He seemed to hear lugubrious howlings and sinister murmurs at night that made his teeth chatter with terror and his hair erect itself under his cotton nightcap. Madame Bernard no more closed an eye than he. And Amanda in her frenzy renounced all thought of the operatic stage and married—for nothing in the world but to quit the paternal lodge—a young barber and hairdresser whom she had never before been able to abide.

At last, one morning, after a more frightful nightmare than usual, Bernard, too, took a great resolution. He went to the proprietor, gave up his keys, and scampered away.

And now on the Rue de la Victoire stands the abandoned house, 'The Accursed House', whose history I have told you. Dust thickens upon the closed slats, grass grows in the court. No tenant ever presents himself now; and in the quarter, where stands this Accursed House, so funereal is its reputation that even the neighbouring houses on either side of it have also depreciated in value.

Lower one's rent! Who would think of such a thing!

New Words

livre:	old French money
documents of succession:	statement in writing saying how somebody wishes his property to be distributed after his death

usury:	practice of lending money at high rates of interest
concierge:	a caretaker, porter in a house or block of flats
deign:	be gracious enough
restraint:	(here) control of oneself
convulsive laughter:	violent fits of laughter
made the rounds:	make one's usual visits (to inspect or make an announcement)
demented:	mad
commotion:	noisy confusion; excitement
sceptic:	person who doubts the truth of a particular claim or theory
sinister:	suggesting evil or the likelihood of coming misfortune
remorse:	deep, bitter regret for wrong-doing
philanthropy:	practical sympathy and benevolence
garret:	room on the top floor of a house, especially in the roof
muffle:	dull the sound of something by wrapping it up in cloth, etc.
defunct:	dead
chiropodist:	person who is expert in the treatment of troubles of the feet and toe-nails
rout:	disorderly retreat
catastrophe:	sudden happening that causes great suffering and destruction
facade:	(here) front of the building
lugubrious:	dismal; mournful; gloomy
frenzy:	violent excitement
scampered:	ran away in fright
depreciated:	became less in value

Comprehension:

1. What event disturbed the smooth, peaceful life of the Vicomte de B——? What important piece of property fell into his hands as a result of this?
2. The Vicomte did not agree with something which his uncle had fixed—can you identify it? He thought the high rent amounted to *usury*. What other word does he use to describe the heavy rent?
3. Which phrase helps you to guess the age of the concierge Bernard? What unexpected order did he receive from his master? What unfortunate consequences did he think would follow if the rents were lowered?
4. Bernard thought that the rents could be reduced only if the lodgers did something—what is it? What did he think had compelled his master to take the fateful decision? On the other hand, what did his wife and daughter think of the Vicomte's decision?
5. Why did Bernard quarrel with his wife? What did Madame Bernard ask of the Vicomte to prove that she was 'a wise and prudent woman'? Did the concierge's family think of disobeying the proprietor's order? What did they decide to do finally?
6. Can you describe the tenants' immediate reaction to Bernard's important announcement? Not all the tenants believed Bernard—what two expressions does the author use to describe such people?
7. 'Then began reflections and commentaries'—What was the question every tenant asked himself? How many floors did the building have? The author says that there was a 'vague disquiet' in the building during this period. What other expression in the same sentence does the author use to suggest the tense atmosphere that prevailed then?
8. What were some of the reasons the tenants offered to explain the proprietor's strange action? Which of these do *you* think was the most improbable? According to the tenants, what extraordinary things began to happen after the rents were lowered?

9. Did the lodgers remain for long after the strange things began to occur? What did they do in their frenzied terror? Why do you think the would-be lodgers fled too? 'Bernard, too, took a great resolution'—What was it?

10. Which word in the last portion of the story tells you that no one stays in the Vicomte's lodge now? Did the lodge's evil reputation affect the neighbouring houses too? How?

Steps to Interpretation

1. Read the opening sentence of the story and look particularly at the word *unfortunately*. Does it indicate what direction the story is going to take? Do the events that follow justify the use of this word? How?
2. The Vicomte says: 'I will begin tomorrow to lower my rents, and my tenants will bless me.' What impression of the man do you get when you read this statement? Do you feel that such a trait as generosity could often prove fatal to the owner?
3. Notice Bernard the concierge. How does he conduct himself in the presence of his master? At home he insists that he should be taken 'seriously in his own lodge'—What does this suggest about his relationship with his wife? Later, when he has to announce his great news to the tenants, why do you think he 'buttons himself into his best frock coat'?
4. When Bernard announces his important news, people in the lodge who were strangers to one another suddenly came together. What does this tell you about the lodgers in particular and about all such people? Do people tend to cluster together in times of trouble or distress?
5. Why do the tenants refuse to think that the Vicomte could have lowered the rents out of sheer generosity? Why do they feel that the proprietor's action is unnatural? In what respect is this story a satire on human nature?

A Day's Wait

Ernest Hemingway

Ernest Hemingway (1899–1961) is a significant name in modern American fiction. The spare, agile style of his novels and short stories has greatly influenced the development of modern prose. His important novels are *The Sun also Rises* (1926), *A Farewell to Arms* (1929), *For Whom the Bell Tolls* (1940) and *The Old Man and the Sea* (1952). In 1954 he was awarded the Nobel Prize for Literature.

'A Day's Wait' is a fascinating story about a boy who believes that he is going to die. When you read the story notice how the little boy reacts to the prospect of death.

He came into the room to shut the windows while we were still in bed and I saw he looked ill. He was shivering, his face was white, and he walked slowly as though it ached to move.

'What's the matter, Schatz?'

'I've got a headache.'

'You better go back to bed.'

'No. I'm all right.'

'You go to bed. I'll see you when I'm dressed.'

But when I came downstairs he was dressed, sitting by the fire, looking a very sick and miserable boy of nine years. When I put my hand on his forehead I knew he had a fever.

'You go up to bed,' I said, 'you're sick.'

'I'm all right,' he said.

When the doctor came he took the boy's temperature.

'What is it?' I asked him.

'One hundred and two.'

Downstairs, the doctor left three different medicines in different coloured capsules with instructions for giving them. One was to bring down the fever, another a purgative, the third to overcome an acid condition. The germs of influenza can only exist in an acid condition, he explained. He seemed to know all about influenza and said there was nothing to worry about if the fever did not go above one hundred and four degrees. This was a light epidemic of flu and there was no danger if you avoided pneumonia.

Back in the room I wrote the boy's temperature down and made a note of the time to give the various capsules.

'Do you want me to read to you?'

'All right. If you want to,' said the boy. His face was very white and there were dark areas under his eyes. He lay still in the bed and seemed very detached from what was going on.

I read aloud from Howard Pyle's *Book of Pirates*; but I could see he was not following what I was reading.

'How do you feel, Schatz?' I asked him.

'Just the same, so far,' he said.

I sat at the foot of the bed and read to myself while I waited for it to be time to give another capsule. It would have been natural for him to go to sleep, but when I looked up he was looking at the foot of the bed, looking very strangely.

'Why don't you try to go to sleep? I'll wake you up for the medicine.'

'I'd rather stay awake.'

After a while he said to me, 'You don't have to stay in here with me, Papa, if it bothers you.'

'It doesn't bother me.'

'No, I mean you don't have to stay if it's going to bother you.'

I thought perhaps he was a little lightheaded and after giving him the prescribed capsules at eleven o'clock I went out for a while.

It was a bright, cold day, the ground covered with a sleet that had frozen so that it seemed as if all the bare trees, the bushes, the cut brush and all the grass and the bare ground had been varnished with ice. I took the young Irish setter for a little walk up the road and along a frozen creek, but it was difficult to stand or walk on the glassy surface and the red dog slipped and slithered and I fell twice, hard, once dropping my gun and having it slide away over the ice.

We flushed a covey of quail under a high clay bank with overhanging brush and I killed two as they went out of sight over the top of the bank. Some of the covey lit in trees, but most of them scattered into brush piles and it was necessary to jump on the ice-coated mounds of brush several times before they would flush. Coming out while you were poised unsteadily on the icy, springy brush they made difficult shooting and I killed two, missed five, and started back pleased to have found a covey close to the house and happy there were so many left to find on another day.

At the house they said the boy had refused to let anyone come into the room.

'You can't come in,' he said. 'You mustn't get what I have.'

I went up to him and found him in exactly the position I had left him, white-faced, but with the tops of his cheeks flushed by the fever staring still, as he had stared, at the foot of the bed.

I took his temperature.

'What is it?'

'Something like a hundred,' I said. It was one hundred and two and four-tenths.

'It was a hundred and two,' he said.

'Who said so?'

'The doctor.'

'Your temperature is all right,' I said. 'It's nothing to worry about.'

'I don't worry,' he said, 'but I can't keep from thinking.'

'Don't think,' I said. 'Just take it easy.'

'I'm taking it easy,' he said and looked straight ahead. He was evidently holding tight onto himself about something.'

'Take this with water.'

'Do you think it will do any good?'

'Of course it will.'

I sat down and opened the Pirate book and commenced to read but I could see he was not following, so I stopped.

'About what time do you think I'm going to die?' he asked.

'What?'

'About how long will it be before I die?'

'You aren't going to die. What's the matter with you?'

'Oh, yes, I am. I heard him say a hundred and two.'

He had been waiting to die all day, ever since nine o'clock in the morning.

'You poor Schatz,' I said. 'Poor old Schatz. It's like miles and kilometres. You aren't going to die. That's a different thermometer. On that thermometer thirty-seven is normal. On this kind it's ninety-eight.'

'Are you sure?'

New Words

shivering:	trembling (here, from fear perhaps)
'you better. . .bed':	the fuller form is 'You had better. . . bed'. It means 'It would be good for you to. . .bed.'
capsule:	a shell or container with medicine
purgative:	medicine that cleanses the bowels
acid condition:	(here) having more than the normal amount of acid in the stomach
light:	(here) mild
epidemic:	a disease, when it becomes wide-spread
pneumonia:	illness with inflammation of the lungs
still:	(here) without sound or movement
detached from:	not interested in, or influenced by
Howard Pyle's *Book of Pirates:*	*The Book of Pirates* is one of the children's storybooks written by Howard Pyle (1853–1911), an American artist and author.
pirate:	sea robber
following:	(here) understanding (what was being read)
bother:	cause trouble or worry
light-headed:	dizzy or delirious
flushed:	become red
take it easy:	(here) don't worry
holding tight onto himself:	keeping his grasp on something; (here) trying to hide a secret

hold over himself: refers to the way Schatz was controlling his tension.

Comprehension

1. Can you guess what time of the day it is when the story opens? Who do you think could be the 'we' in the first sentence?
2. What are the indications that Schatz is ill? What does he think is the matter with himself? Can this be the reason why he thinks it is all right to go out with his father? How old is he at the time of this story?
3. Who says 'one hundred and two'? What does he mean by it? The doctor leaves three different medicines—why? He thinks the father should begin to worry only after a certain stage—at which stage? Which does he think is more dangerous, flu or pneumonia?
4. Does Schatz himself ask his father to read to him? Do you think the father reads to the boy every day? Does Schatz enjoy the story? Why not? Why do you think he seems very detached from what is going on round him?
5. Does Schatz go to sleep after taking the first capsule? What does he do instead? Why does he not want his father to stay in the room with him? What makes the father think that the boy is a little light-headed?
6. Schatz does not allow people into his room. Why? What does the thermometer show the second time? Has the temperature risen?
7. Why does Schatz ask what time he is going to die? Does he think he is going to die because he has been told so by the boys in school? In what way has he misunderstood what they told him?
8. 'It's like miles and kilometres.' What does *it* refer to? What are the two kinds of thermometers mentioned by the author. How does the father prove his point that there are two kinds of thermometers?
9. What is the first indication that Schatz has realised his mistake? What do you think happened the next day?

10. What is his state of mind at the end of the story? Is this why he cries so easily at little things?

Steps to Interpretation

1. The boy refuses to go back to bed and insists that he is all right. Is he being disobedient? What trait of his character does this reveal?
2. What picture of the doctor do you get from the manner in which he talks to Schatz's father?
3. Schatz says: 'I'm taking it easy.' Is this true? How does the father realise that his son is not taking it easy? 'Take *this* with water'—what can it be?
4. There is practically no mention of any character other than Schatz and his father. Do you think this is deliberate on the part of the author? In what way does this feature intensify the father-son relationship?
5. Schatz is a boy with delicate feelings. Do you think that the author has succeeded in describing his highly sensitive nature? Why do you think so? Do you think all children of Schatz's age are as sensitive?

Marriage is a Private Affair

Chinua Achebe

Chinua Achebe is Nigeria's best known writer and probably the most distinguished writer of fiction from Africa. Educated at Government College, Umuahia, and later at University College, Ibadan, he joined the Nigerian Broadcasting Corporation in 1954. At the moment he works at the Institute of African Studies at Nsukka. The best-known among his novels are *Things Fall Apart* (1958), *No Longer at Ease* (1960), *Arrow of God* (1964) and *A Man of the People* (1966). Achebe has also distinguished himself as a poet; his collection of poems, *Beware Soul Brothers*, won the Commonwealth poetry prize in 1972.

Achebe is deeply interested in the beliefs and traditions of the Ibo people—the tribe to which he himself belongs. In *Marriage is a Private Affair*, a story he wrote while he was a student at Ibadan, he talks about two young people in love who try to break away from social traditions and pressures.

'Have you written to your dad yet?' asked Nene one afternoon as she sat with Nnaemeka in her room at 16 Kasanga Street, Lagos.

'No. I've been thinking about it. I think it's better to tell him when I get home on leave!'

'But why? Your leave is such a long way off yet—six whole weeks. He should be let into our happiness now.'

Nnaemeka was silent for a while, and then began very slowly as if he groped for his words: 'I wish I were sure it would be happiness to him.'

'Of course it must,' replied Nene, a little surprised. 'Why shouldn't it?'

'You have lived in Lagos all your life, and you know very little about people in remote parts of the country.'

'That's what you always say. But I don't believe anybody will be so unlike other people that they will be unhappy when their sons are engaged to marry.'

'Yes. They are most unhappy if the engagement is not arranged by them. In our case it's worse—you are not even an Ibo.'

This was said so seriously and so bluntly that Nene could not find speech immediately. In the cosmopolitan atmosphere of the city it had always seemed to her something of a joke that a person's tribe could determine whom he married.

At last she said, 'You don't really mean that he will object to your marrying me simply on that account? I had always thought you Ibos were kindly disposed to other people.'

'So we are. But when it comes to marriage, well, it's not quite so simple. And this,' he added, 'is not peculiar to the Ibos. If your father were alive and lived in the heart of Ibibo-land he would be exactly like my father.'

'I don't know. But anyway, as your father is so fond of you, I'm sure he will forgive you soon enough. Come on then, be a good boy and send him a nice lovely letter. . .'

'It would not be wise to break the news to him by writing. A letter will bring it upon him with a shock. I'm quite sure about that.'

'All right, honey, suit yourself. You know your father.'

As Nnaemeka walked home that evening he turned over in his mind different ways of overcoming his father's opposition, especially now that he had gone and found a girl for him. He had thought of showing his letter to Nene but decided on second thoughts not to, at least for the moment. He read it again when he got home and couldn't help smiling to himself. He remembered Ugoye quite well, an Amazon of a girl who used to beat up all the boys, himself included, on the way to the stream, a complete dunce at school.

> 'I have found a girl who will suit you admirably—Ugoye Nweke, the eldest daughter of our neighbour, Jacob Nweke. She has a proper Christian upbringing. When she stopped schooling some years ago, her father (a man of sound judgment) sent her to live in the house of a pastor where she has received all the training a wife could need. Her Sunday School teacher has told me that she reads her Bible very fluently. I hope we shall begin negotiations when you come home in December.'

On the second evening of his return from Lagos Nnaemeka sat with his father under a cassia tree. This was the old man's retreat where he went to read his Bible when the parching December sun had set and a fresh, reviving wind blew on the leaves.

'Father,' began Nnaemeka suddenly, 'I have come to ask for forgiveness.'

'Forgiveness? For what, my son?' he asked in amazement.

'It's about this marriage question.'

'Which marriage question?'

'I can't—we must—I mean it is impossible for me to marry Nweke's daughter.'

'Impossible? Why?' asked his father.

'I don't love her.'

'Nobody said you did. Why should you?' he asked.

'Marriage today is different. . .'

'Look here, my son,' interrupted his father, 'nothing is different. What one looks for in a wife are a good character and a Christian background.'

Nnaemeka saw there was no hope along the present line of argument.

'Moreover,' he said, 'I am engaged to marry another girl who has all of Ugoye's good qualities, and who. . .'

His father did not believe his ears. 'What did you say?' he asked slowly and disconcertingly.

'She is a good Christian,' his son went on, 'and a teacher in a Girls' School in Lagos.'

'Teacher, did you say? If you consider that a qualification for a good wife I should like to point out to you, Nnaemeka, that no Christian woman should teach. St. Paul in his letter to the Corinthians says that women should keep silence.' He rose slowly from his seat and paced forwards and backwards. This was his pet subject, and he condemned vehemently those church leaders who encouraged women to teach in their schools. After he had spent his emotion on a long homily he at last came back to his son's engagement, in a seemingly milder tone.

'Whose daughter is she, anyway?'

'She is Nene Atang.'

'What!' All the mildness was gone again. 'Did you say Nene Atang, what does that mean?'

'Nene Atang from Calabar. She is the only girl I can marry.' This was a very rash reply and Nnaemeka expected the storm to burst. But it did not. His father merely walked away into his room. This was most unexpected and perplexed Nnaemeka. His father's silence was infinitely more menacing than a flood of threatening speech. That night the old man did not eat.

When he sent for Nnaemeka a day later he applied all possible ways of dissuasion. But the young man's heart was hardened, and his father eventually gave him up as lost.

'I owe it to you, my son, as a duty to show you what is right and what is wrong. Whoever put this idea into your head might as well have cut your throat. It is Satan's work.' He waved his son away.

'You will change your mind, Father, when you know Nene.'

'I shall never see her,' was the reply. From that night the father scarcely spoke to his son. He did not, however, cease hoping that he would realise how serious was the danger he was heading for. Day and night he put him in his prayers.

Nnaemeka, for his own part, was very deeply affected by his father's grief. But he kept hoping that it would pass away. If it had occurred to him that never in the history of his people had a man married a woman who spoke a different tongue, he might have been less optimistic. 'It has never been heard,' was the verdict of an old man speaking a few weeks later. In that short sentence he spoke for all of his people. This man had come with others to commiserate with Okeke when news went round about his son's behaviour. By that time the son had gone back to Lagos.

'It has never been heard,' said the old man again with a sad shake of his head.

'What did Our Lord say?' asked another gentleman.

'Sons shall rise against their Fathers; it is there in the Holy Book.'

'It is the beginning of the end,' said another.

The discussion thus tending to become theological, Madubogwu, a highly practical man, brought it down once more to the ordinary level.

'Have you thought of consulting a native doctor about your son?' he asked Nnaemeka's father.

'He isn't sick,' was the reply.

'What is he then? The boy's mind is diseased and only a good herbalist can bring him back to his right senses. The medicine he requires is Amalile, the same that women apply with success to recapture their husbands' straying affection.'

'Madubogwu is right,' said another gentleman. 'This thing calls for medicine.'

'I shall not call in a native doctor.' Nnaemeka's father was known to be obstinately ahead of his more superstitious neighbours in these matters. 'I will not be another Mrs Ochuba. If my son wants to kill himself let him do it with his own hands. It is not for me to help him.'

'But it was her fault,' said Madubogwu. 'She ought to have gone to an honest herbalist. She was a clever woman, nevertheless.'

'She was a wicked murderess,' said Jonathan who rarely argued with his neighbours because, he often said, they were incapable of reasoning. 'The medicine was prepared for her husband, it was his name they called in its preparation and I am sure it would have been perfectly beneficial to him. It was wicked to put it into the herbalist's food, and say you were only trying it out.'

Six months later, Nnaemeka was showing his young wife a short letter from his father:

'It amazes me that you could be so unfeeling as to send me your wedding picture. I would have sent it back. But on further thought I decided just to cut off your wife and send it back to you because I have nothing to do with her. How I wish that I had nothing to do with you either.'

When Nene read through this letter and looked at the mutilated picture her eyes filled with tears, and she began to sob.

'Don't cry, my darling,' said her husband. 'He is essentially good-natured and will one day look more kindly on our marriage.' But years passed and that one day did not come.

For eight years, Okeke would have nothing to do with his son, Nnaemeka. Only three times (when Nnaemeka asked to come home and spend his leave) did he write to him.

'I can't have you in my house,' he replied on one occasion. 'It can be of no interest to me where or how you spend your leave—or your life, for that matter.'

The prejudice against Nnaemeka's marriage was not confined to his little village. In Lagos, especially among his people who worked there, it showed itself in a different way. Their women, when they met at their village meeting, were not hostile to Nene. Rather, they paid her such excessive deference as to make her feel she was not one of them. But as time went on, Nene gradually broke through some of this prejudice and even began to make friends among them. Slowly and grudgingly they began to admit that she kept her home much better than most of them.

The story eventually got to the little village in the heart of the Ibo country that Nnaemeka and his young wife were a most happy couple. But his father was one of the few people in the village who knew nothing about this. He always displayed so much temper whenever his son's name was mentioned that everyone avoided it in his presence. By a tremendous effort of will he had succeeded in pushing his son to the back of his mind. The strain had nearly killed him but he had persevered, and won.

Then one day he received a letter from Nene, and in spite of himself he began to glance through it perfunctorily until all of a sudden the expression on his face changed and he began to read more carefully:

> . . . . .Our two sons, from the day they learnt that they have a grandfather, have insisted on being taken to him. I find it impossible to tell them that you will not see them. I implore you to allow Nnaemeka to bring them home for a short time during his leave next month. I shall remain here in Lagos. . . .'

The old man at once felt the resolution he had built up over so many years falling in. He was telling himself that he must not give in. He tried to steel his heart against all emotional appeals. It was a re-enactment of that other struggle. He leaned against a window and looked out. The sky was overcast with heavy black clouds and a high wind began to blow filling the air with dust and dry leaves. It was one of those rare occasions when even Nature takes a hand in a human fight. Very soon it began to rain, the first rain in the year. It came down in large sharp drops and was accompanied by the lightning and thunder which mark a change of season. Okeke was trying hard not to think of his two grandsons. But he knew he was now fighting a losing battle. He tried to hum a favourite hymn but the pattering of large raindrops on the roof broke up the tune. His mind immediately returned to the children. How could he shut his door against them? By a curious mental process he imagined them standing, sad and forsaken, under the harsh angry weather—shut out from his house.

That night he hardly slept, from remorse—and a vague fear that he might die without making it up to them.

New Words

grope for words:	search for words
bluntly:	plainly; not troubling to be polite
cosmopolitan:	free from prejudices
Amazon:	strong, manlike woman
retreat:	place for quiet and rest
disconcertingly:	in an upsetting manner
vehemently:	strongly
homily:	sermon: long tedious talk
menacing:	dangerous
commiserate:	sympathize
herbalist:	the 'medicine man'
deference:	respect
perfunctorily:	done as a duty, but without care or interest
steel his heart:	harden his heart
remorse:	deep, bitter regret for wrong-doing.

Comprehension

1. 'Have you written to your dad yet?' What did Nene want Nnaemeka to write his father about? Does Nnaemeka want to write? How else does he want to break the news to his father?
2. Why would Nnaemeka's father be unhappy if the son wrote to him about the engagement? Why would it be worse in Nene's case?
3. Who did Nnaemeka's father choose as a bride for his son? Did Nnaemeka know the girl? What did he remember of her? Did he like her? What qualities of hers appealed to Nnaemeka's father?
4. 'Nnaemeka saw there was no hope along the present line of argument.' What was his first line of argument? What was the next? Did it succeed? What was his father's counter-argument?

5. How did Nnaemeka's father react when the son said, 'She is the only girl I can marry'? Did he shout at the young man? How did he show his anger? How did his father's grief affect Nnaemeka? What did he hope? Why was he optimistic?
6. Why did the old men of the tribe say that it was 'the beginning of the end'? What did one of them suggest to cure Nnaemeka of his 'disease'? How did Nnaemeka's father reject the idea?
7. What had Mrs Ochuba done? Can you reconstruct the story from the conversation of Jonathan and the others?
8. What did Nnaemeka's father do to his son's wedding photograph? How did the mutilated picture affect Nene? What did Nnaemeka still hope?
9. How did the Ibo women in Lagos treat Nene? How did Nene make friends among them? Were the young couple happy? Did the old man know of this? Why?
10. What did Nene write to the old man? How did the letter affect him? Love towards his son had not softened the old man's heart. What did it at last?

Steps to Interpretation

1. Nene was suprised that Nnaemeka's father would be unhappy to hear about his son's engagement to her. There are other examples in the story of how her urban upbringing had influenced her views and opinions. Can you find a few of them?
2. 'If your father were alive and lived in the heart of Ibibo-land he would be exactly like my father.' What trait of Nnaemeka's character is revealed by these words?
3. Read the letter Nnaemeka's father wrote to his son. What picture of the old man emerges out of the letter? Would you have been angry with him if you were his son?
4. 'He is essentially good-natured.' Do you agree with Nnaemeka's assessment of his father? Why?

5. What picture of the Ibo people do you get from this story? Are they superstitious? What beliefs and principles guide them? Are they changing? Is Nnaemeka's father just one of his tribe, or is he different? Are we superstitious? How do our superstitions rule our lives? Why do you think people have superstitions?
6. Nnaemeka's father is against his son's marriage to Nene because they belong to different tribes. Do you find similar situations in India? What would you have done if you were in Nnaemeka's or Nene's position?—in Nnaemeka's father's position?
7. Do you think two people who belong to different languages or culture groups should not marry?
8. Is marriage a private affair? How are other people involved?

The Ransom of Red Chief

O. Henry

O. Henry (1862–1910) was the pen-name of the famous American short story writer, William Sidney Porter. When he was three O. Henry's mother (from whom he had inherited tuberculosis and a talent for painting) died, pushing the little boy into a very unsettled childhood. He was in turn a cartoonist, a labourer, a journalist and a cashier in a bank. Falsely convicted for embezzlement of money, O. Henry spent several years in prison. Some of his best stories were written while in prison. By the time he left prison he was a famous writer. He wrote at the astonishing rate of fifty or sixty stories a year. In all he wrote about six hundred stories which are collected mainly in four volumes: *The Four Million, The Voice of the City, Sixes and Sevens* and *Waifs and Strays*.

His stories are famous for 'their humanity, humour, compassion and irony', and for the unexpected twist in the ending of which *The Ransom of Red Chief* is a superb example.

It looked like a good thing; but wait till I tell you. We were down South, in Alabama—Bill Driscoll and myself—when this kidnapping idea struck us.

There was a town down there, as flat as a cake, and called Summit, of course.

Bill and I had a joint capital of about six hundred dollars, and we needed just two thousand dollars to buy some land. We talked it over on the front step of the hotel. Love of children, we said, was strong in country people; therefore, and for other reasons, a kidnapping plan ought to do better there than in a city. We knew that the town couldn't get after us with anything stronger than a few constables and, maybe, some lazy dogs and an article or two in the *Weekly Farmers' Newspaper*. So, it looked good.

We chose for our victim the only child of an important citizen named Ebenezer Dorset. The father was respectable and mean, a man in the building trade and a strict, upright man. The kid was a boy of ten, with freckles, and hair the colour of the cover of the magazine you buy when you want to catch a train. Bill and me thought that Ebenezer would offer a ransom of at least two thousand dollars. But wait till I tell you.

About two miles from Summit was a little mountain, covered with thick wood. At the back of this mountain was a cave. There we stored food.

One evening, after sunset, we drove in a cart past old Dorset's house. The kid was in the street, throwing rocks at a kitten on the opposite fence.

'Hey, little boy!' said Bill, 'would you like to have a bag of sweets and a nice ride?'

The boy hit Bill neatly in the eye with a piece of brick.

'That will cost the old man an extra five hundred dollars,' said Bill, climbing down.

That boy put up a fight like a middle-sized bear; but, at last, we got him down in the bottom of the cart and drove away. We took him up to the cave, and I tied the horse up in the wood. After dark I drove the cart to the little village, three miles away, where we had hired it, and walked back to the mountain.

Bill was putting plaster over the scratches and cuts on his face. There was a fire burning behind the high rock at the entrance of the cave, and the boy was watching a pot of boiling coffee, with two feathers stuck in his red hair. He pointed a stick at me when I came up, and said:

'Ha! do you dare enter the camp of Red Chief, the terror of the plains?'

'He's all right now,' said Bill, rolling up his trousers and examining some cuts on his legs. 'We're playing Indians, and we'll give the kid the show of his lifetime.'

Yes, sir, that boy seemed to be having the time of his life. The fun of camping out in a cave made him forget that he was prisoner himself. He immediately named me Snake-eye, the Spy, and announced that I was to be burned at the rising of the sun.

Then we had supper, and he filled his mouth full of meat and began to talk. He made a during-dinner speech something like this:

'I like this fine. I never camped out before; but I had a pet wild cat once, and I was nine last birthday. I hate to go to school. Rats ate up sixteen of Jimmy Talbot's aunt's hen's eggs. Are there any real Indians in this wood? I want some more meat. Does the trees moving make the wind blow? We had five puppies. What makes your nose so red, Hank? My father has lots of money. Are the stars hot? I beat Ed Walker twice, Saturday. I don't like girls. You can't catch toads unless with a string. Do oxen make any noise? Why are oranges round? Have you got beds to sleep on in this cave? Amos Murray has got six toes. A parrot can talk, but a monkey or fish can't. How many does it take to make twelve?'

Every minute he would remember that he was an Indian and pick up his stick rifle and go softly to the mouth of the cave to search for the spies of the enemy. Now and then he would let out a war cry that was a terror to Bill. That boy had Bill frightened from the start.

'Red Chief,' said I to the kid, 'would you like to go home?'

'Aw, what for?' said he. 'I don't have any fun at home. I hate to go to school. I like to camp out. You won't take me back home again, Snake-eye, will you?'

'Not right away,' said I. 'We'll stay in the cave for a while.'

'All right,' said he. 'That'll be fine. I never had such fun in all my life.'

We went to bed about eleven o'clock. We spread down some wide, thick blankets and put Red Chief between us. We weren't afraid he would run away. He kept us awake for three hours, jumping up and reaching for his stick rifle and crying out, 'Listen, friend,' in mine and Bill's ears, as any fancied noise told his young imagination of the secret approach of enemies. At last I fell into a troubled sleep and dreamed that I had been kidnapped and chained to a tree by a fierce robber with red hair.

Just at daybreak, I was awakened by awful screams from Bill. They weren't cries or shouts such as you'd expect from a man. They were simply indecent, terrifying, humiliating screams, such as women would give out when they see ghosts or cockroaches. It's an awful thing to hear a strong, desperate, fat man scream suddenly in a cave at daybreak.

I jumped up to see what the matter was. Red Chief was sitting on Bill's chest, with one hand twisted in Bill's hair. In the other he had the sharp knife we used for cutting meat; and he was very carefully trying to take the skin and hair off Bill's head, according to the punishment that had been laid upon him the evening before.

I got the knife away from the kid, and made him lie

down again. But, from that moment, Bill's spirit was broken. He lay down on his side of the bed, but he never closed an eye again in sleep as long as that boy was with us. I went to sleep for a while, but suddenly I remembered that Red Chief had said I was to be burned at the rising of the sun. I wasn't nervous or afraid; but I sat up and lit my pipe and leaned against a rock.

'What are you getting up so soon for, Sam?' asked Bill

'Me?' said I. 'Oh, I got a kind of pain in my shoulder. I thought sitting up would rest it.'

'You're a liar!' said Bill. 'You're afraid. You were to be burned at sunrise, and you were afraid he would do it. And he would too, if he could find a match. Isn't it awful, Sam? Do you think anybody will pay out money to get a little wretch like that back home?'

'Sure,' said I. 'A noisy kid like that is just the kind that parents love. Now, you and the Chief get up and cook breakfast, while I go up on the top of this mountain and have a look around.'

When I got back to the cave I found Bill up against the side of it, breathing hard, and the boy threatening to smash him with a rock half as big as a coconut.

'He put a red-hot boiled potato down my back,' explained Bill, 'and then stood on it with his foot; and I hit him. Have you got a gun on you, Sam?'

I took the rock away from the boy and kind of stopped the argument. 'I'll finish you,' said the kid to Bill. 'No man ever struck the Red Chief but he got punished for it. You better watch out.'

After breakfast the kid took a piece of leather with strings wrapped around it out of his pocket and went outside the cave unwinding it.

'What's he up to now?' said Bill anxiously. 'You don't think he'll run away, do you, Sam?'

'No fear of it,' said I. 'He doesn't seem to be very fond of home. But we've got to fix up some plan about the ransom. There doesn't seem to be much excitement in Summit about his disappearance; but maybe they haven't discovered that the wolves have carried away the tender lamb. (Heaven help the wolves!) His people may think that he's spending the night with Aunt Jane or one of the neighbours. Anyhow, he'll be missed today. Tonight we must get a message to his father demanding the two thousand dollars for his return.'

Just then we heard a kind of war-cry. It was a sling that Red Chief had pulled out of his pocket and he was twisting it round his head.

I jumped, and heard a heavy sound and a kind of sigh from Bill, like the one a horse gives out when you take his saddle off. A rock the size of an egg had caught Bill just behind his left ear. He ran around like a mad man all over the place and fell in the fire across the frying-pan of hot water for washing the dishes. I dragged him out and poured cold water on his head for half an hour.

I went out and caught that boy and shook him until I couldn't shake him any more.

'If you don't behave,' said I, 'I'll take you straight home. Now, are you going to be good or not?'

'It was only for fun,' said he. 'I didn't mean to hurt old Hank. But what did he hit me for? I'll behave, Snake-eye, if you won't send me home, and if you'll let me play the Black Scout today.'

'I don't know the game,' said I. 'That's for you and Mr Bill to decide. He's your playmate for the day. I'm going away for a while, on business. Now, you come and make friends with him and say you are sorry for hurting him, or home you go, at once.'

I made him and Bill shake hands, and then I took Bill

aside and told him I was going to Poplar Cove, a little village three miles from the cave, and find out what I could about how the kidnapping had been regarded in Summit. Also, I thought it best to send a sharp letter to old man Dorset that day, demanding the ransom and telling him how it should be paid.

'You won't leave me long with this wretch, will you, Sam?' asked Bill.

'I'll be back sometime this afternoon,' said I. 'You must keep the boy amused and quiet till I return. And now we'll write the letter to old Dorset.'

Bill and I got paper and pencil and worked on the letter while Red Chief, with a blanket wrapped round him, walked up and down, guarding the mouth of the cave. Bill begged me tearfully to make the ransom fifteen hundred dollars instead of two thousand. 'I'm not attempting,' said he, 'to forget the moral goodness of parental love, but we're dealing with humans, and it isn't human for anybody to give up two thousand dollars for that forty-pound piece of freckled wildcat. I'm willing to take a chance at fifteen hundred dollars, and I'll give you the difference.'

So, to relieve Bill, I agreed, and together we wrote a letter that ran this way:

Ebenezer Dorset, Esq:

We are keeping your boy in a place far from Summit. It is useless for you or the most skilled detectives to attempt to find him. The only terms on which you can have him back are these: we demand fifteen hundred dollars in large bills for his return; the money to be left at midnight tonight at the same spot and in the same box as your reply—as hereinafter described. If you agree to these terms, send your answer in writing by a single messenger tonight at half past eight o'clock.

After crossing Owl Creek, on the road to Poplar Cove, there are three large trees about a hundred yards apart, close to the fence of the wheat field on the right-hand side. At the bottom of the fence post, opposite the third tree, will be found a small cardboard box.

The messenger will place the answer in this box and return immediately to Summit.

If you try to inform the police or fail to agree with our demand as stated, you will never see your boy again.

If you pay the money as demanded, he will be returned to you safe and well within three hours. These terms are final, and if you do not agree to them, no further letter will be sent.

TWO DESPERATE MEN.

I addressed the letter to Dorset, and put it in my pocket. As I was about to start, the kid came up to me and said, 'Aw, Snake-eye, you said I could play the Black Scout while you were gone.'

'Play it, of course,' said I. 'Mr Bill will play with you. What kind of game is it?'

'I'm the Black Scout,' said the Red Chief, 'and I have to ride to the village to warn the people that the Indians are coming. I'm tired of playing Indian myself. I want to be the Black Scout.'

'All right,' said I. 'It sounds harmless to me. I expect Mr Bill will help you defeat the Indians.'

'What am I do to?' asked Bill.

'You're the horse,' said the Black Scout. 'Get down on your hands and knees. How can I ride to the village without a horse?'

'You'd better keep him interested,' said I, 'till we get the plan going.'

Bill got down on all fours, and a look came in his eye like a rabbit's when you catch it in a trap.

'How far is it to the village, kid?' he asked in a strange manner of voice.

'Ninety miles,' said the Black Scout. 'And you have to go fast to get there in time. Get on, now!'

The Black Scout jumped on Bill's back and dug his heels in his side.

'For heaven's sake,' said Bill, 'hurry back, Sam, as soon as you can. I wish we hadn't made the ransom more than a thousand. Say, you stop kicking me or I will get up and kick you.'

I walked to Poplar Cove and sat around the post-office and store, talking with the old ones who came in for buying things. One bearded old man said that he heard Summit was all upset about old Ebenezer Dorset's boy having been lost or stolen. That was all I wanted to know. I bought some smoking tobacco, referred to the price of peas, posted my letter secretly and came away.

When I got back to the cave Bill and the boy were not be found. I looked around the cave and risked a shout or two, but there was no reply.

So I lighted my pipe and sat down on a grassy bank to await developments.

In about half an hour I heard some noise in the bushes and Bill came out. Behind him was the kid, stepping softly like a scout with a broad grin on his face. Bill stopped, took off his hat and wiped his face with a red handkerchief. The kid stopped about eight feet behind him.

'Sam,' said Bill, 'I suppose you'll think I'm a fool, but I could not help it. The boy is gone; I have sent him home. All is off. I tried to be faithful to our agreement; but there came a limit.'

'What's the trouble, Bill?' I asked him.

'I was ridden,' said Bill, 'the ninety miles to the village not missing an inch. And then for an hour, I had to try and explain to him why there was nothing in holes, how a road can run both ways, and what makes grass green. I tell you, Sam, a human can stand only so much. I took him by his collar and dragged him down the mountain. On the way he kicked my legs black and blue from the knees down; and I have two or three bites on my thumb and hand.'

'But he's gone,' continued Bill, 'gone home. I showed him the road to Summit and kicked him about eight feet nearer there at one kick. I'm sorry we lose the ransom; but it was either that or Bill Driscoll to the madhouse.'

'Bill,' said I, 'there isn't any heart disease in your family, is there?

'No,' said Bill, 'nothing like that except malaria and accidents. Why?

'Then you might turn around,' said I, 'and have a look behind you.'

Bill turned and saw the boy, and lost his colour and sat down right on the ground and began to pick aimlessly at grass and little sticks. For an hour I was afraid he might lose his mind. And then I told him that my plan was to put the whole business through immediately and that we would get the ransom and be off with it by midnight, if old Dorset agreed to our terms. So Bill improved enough to give the kid a weak sort of smile and a promise to play the Russian in a Japanese war with him as soon as he felt a little better.

At half past eight I was up in the tree, as well hidden as a tree toad, waiting for the messenger to arrive.

Exactly on time, a half-grown boy rode up the road on a bicycle, found the cardboard box at the foot of the fence-post, slipped a folded piece of paper into it and pedalled away again, back towards Summit.

I waited an hour, and then decided the thing was all right. I slid down the tree, got the note, slipped along the fence till I got to the woods, and was back at the cave in another half an hour. I opened the note, got near the lamp and read it to Bill. It was written with a pen in an awkward hand, and it read:

Two Desperate Men:

Gentlemen, I received your letter today by post, about the ransom you ask for the return of my son. I think you are a little high in your demands, and I hereby make you a proposal, which I am sure you will accept. You bring Johnny home and pay me two hundred and fifty dollars in cash, and I agree to take him off your hands. You had better come at night, for the neighbours believe he is lost. I couldn't be responsible for what they would do to anybody they saw bringing him back.

Very respectfully,
EBENEZER DORSET.

'Good God!' said I, 'of all the rude—'

But I looked at Bill, and hesitated. He had the most appealing look in his eyes I ever saw on the face of a dumb or talking animal.

'Sam,' said he, 'What's two hundred and fifty dollars after all? We've got the money. One more night of this will send me to the madhouse. Besides being a thorough gentleman, I think Mr Dorset is generous for making us such an offer. You aren't going to let the chance go, are you?'

'To tell you the truth, Bill,' said I, 'this little lamb has somewhat got on my nerves too. We'll take him home, pay the ransom and get away from here.'

We took him home that night. We got him to go by telling him that his father had bought a silver rifle and special Indian clothes for him, and we were going to hunt bears the next day.

It was just twelve o'clock when we knocked at Ebenezer's front door. Just at the moment I should have been taking the fifteen hundred dollars from the box under the tree, according to the original plan, Bill was counting out two hundred and fifty dollars into Dorset's hand.

When the kid found out we were going to leave him at home he started up a scream like a horrible wind and clung to Bill's leg. His father dragged him off gradually, like a plaster.

'How long can you hold him?' asked Bill.

'I'm not as strong as I used to be,' said old Dorset, 'but I think I can promise you ten minutes.'

'Enough,' said Bill. 'In ten minutes I shall cross the Central, Southern and Middle Western States, and be running beautifully for the Canadian border.'

And, as dark as it was, and as fat as Bill was, and as good a runner as I am, he was a good mile and half out of Summit before I could catch up with him.

[*Slightly adapted*]

New Words

kidnap:	carry away somebody by force in order to get money (as ransom for his return)
victim:	person suffering from the result of an action
freckles:	small, light brown spots on the face
Indians:	(Red) Indians were the original people of America
toad:	frog-like animal that lives on land
humiliate:	make one feel ashamed
wretch:	miserable person

sling:	strip of leather used for throwing stones to a distance
terms:	conditions
appealing:	moving the feelings
has got on my nerves:	irritates me
cling:	hold tight

Comprehension

1. 'A kidnapping plan ought to do better in the country than in the city.' Why did Sam and Bill think so?
2. How did the two men get the boy into the cart? Was it easy? What did Bill suffer in the attempt?
3. Who did the boy imagine he was? How did he change his mind later? How did the change affect Bill?
4. 'That boy had Bill frightened from the start.' How? In what way did this affect the course of the story?
5. 'Do you think anybody would pay out money to get a little wretch like that back home?' What was Sam's reply? Who was right, Sam or Bill?
6. 'Have you got a gun on you, Sam?' What did Bill want to do with the gun?
7. What was Sam's plan to collect the ransom?
8. What did Bill tell Sam when the latter returned from Poplar Cave? What made him do what he did?
9. 'Bill,' said Sam, 'there isn't any heart disease in your family, is there?' Why did Sam ask this question?
10. What was Mr Dorset's counter-offer to the Two Desperate Men? Why did they accept it?

Interpretation

1. Suppose Sam and Bill were not frightened of the little boy. How do you think the story would have ended?
2. Kidnappers are usually tough and ruthless people. Were Sam and Bill of this kind? Which incidents tell you this?

3. 'There was a town down there, as flat as a cake, and called Summit, of course.' O. Henry is playing with the word 'summit'. Can you explain the humour? Can you spot other instances of similar humorous touches in the story?
4. 'The boy put up a fight like a middle-sized bear. There are numerous instances of similes and metaphors in the story. ('. . . .humiliating screams, such as women would give out when they see ghosts or cockroaches'). Collect a few of them.
5. O. Henry is often called a master of surprise ending. How surprising is the ending of this story? How does O. Henry build up the surprise? Compare this story with 'Fur' by Saki.

Sparrows

K. A. Abbas

K. A. Abbas (b.1914) is one of the distinguished writers in India today. His versatile mind has found expression in diverse spheres of activity. As a journalist he has focussed public attention upon many burning problems of Indian politics and social life. He has also breathed a new life into our film world. But his enduring reputation is mainly based on his two volumes of short stories—*Rice and other Stories* and *One Thousand Nights on a Bed of Stone*. His stories are illumined by his insight into human character, particularly, the poor and the downtrodden.

Sparrows reveals a young man who, thwarted in his ambitions and his love, becomes hardened into a beast and is ultimately reformed by the actions of two sparrows and their young ones.

The sun was setting behind the mango grove which fringed the western extremity of the village when Rahim Khan returned from the fields. Broad and strong despite his fifty odd years, with the plough on his shoulders, and driving his two oxen, he walked through the main street of the village with a haughty and unfriendly air. As he approached the chaupal where a dozen or so peasants were collected for their evening smoke, the hilarious tones of gossip died down to cautious whispers. It was only when he had vanished round the corner and the heavy tread of his footsteps was heard no more that Kallu, passing the communal hookah to another, remarked, 'There goes the hard-hearted devil.' to which Nanha, the fat sweetseller, added: 'He is getting worse and worse every day. Only yesterday he beat poor Ramoo's child for throwing a pebble at his oxen.' Ramnath, the officious zaildar, volunteered further details of Rahim Khan's recent cruelties. 'And the other day he very nearly killed my mare for straying into his field.' The zaildar, of course, thought it quite irrelevant to mention that the straying of his mare had been specially planned by his own mischievous sons. The old grey-haired patel was, as usual, the last to open his toothless mouth. And as usual, his words were prefaced by a pious invocation to the Almighty. 'Hari Ram! Hari Ram!' he muttered, 'I have never seen such a cruel man. He has compassion neither for the child nor for the helpless animal. No wonder is own sons have run away from home.'

The subject of their conversation, meanwhile, had reached his hut which, almost symbolically, stood gaunt and aloof, at a distance from the neighbouring cluster of houses. Leaning the plough up against the low wall of his house, he proceeded to tie the oxen to a pair of big wooden stakes embedded in the ground just in front of the doorway.

'Bhai Rahim Khan!' an obsequious voice said behind him as he was about to enter the house.

'What is it?' he gruffly queried, turning round to address the old woman who had come out of the house nearest his own. As she hesitated to speak he fired a volley of questions: 'What is it? I won't eat you. Why don't you speak, woman? Has your son been arrested again for revenue arrears or has your daughter-in-law delivered another baby?'

As he stopped for breath, the woman summoned up all her courage to utter two words, 'Your wife. . . .' '. . .has run away. . .' He completed the sentence with a grin, which broadened with the realisation that he had guessed right.

'No, no,' the woman hastily explained with an apologetic look, as if she herself were responsible for his wife's absence. 'She has only gone to her brother at Nurpur and will be back in a few days.'

'Bah!' he flung back at her, opening the door. He knew that his wife would never come back.

Seething with inward wrath he entered the dark hut and sat down on the charpoy. A cat mewed in a corner. Finding no one else on whom to vent his anger he flung it out, slamming the door with violence.

There was no one to give him water to wash his dust-laden feet and hands, no one to give him supper, no one whom he could curse and beat. Rahim Khan felt uncomfortable and unhappy. He had always been angry with his wife when she was there, but her absence angered him still more.

'So she's gone,' he mused, lying down on the cot, having decided to go to sleep without his food. During the thirty years of their married life he had always felt that she would leave him one day and, at one time he had even hoped she would. Six years ago, his eldest son Bundu had run away from home because of a more than usually severe beating. Three years later, the younger one, Nuru, joined his brother. Since that day, Rahim Khan felt sure his wife too would run away to her brother's house. But now that she had gone, he felt unhappy—not sorry, no, for he had never loved his wife—but only uncomfortable, as if a necessary piece of furniture had been removed. With her gone, on whom could he shower the outpourings of an embittered heart?

For thirty years his wife had been both the symbol and target of all his grievances against family, against society, against life.

As a youth there had been none in the village to beat

him in feats of athletic skill–in wrestling, in kabaddi, in diving from the canal bridge. He had loved a girl, and had wanted to join a touring circus which happened to pass through the village. In the circus, he had felt, lay the key to his ambitions—a career after his own heart—travel-fame. And in Radha, the daughter of Ram Charan, the village banya, he thought he had found his soul-mate. He had first noticed her watching him at a wrestling match and it had been the greatest moment of his life when, standing up after vanquishing his adversary, he had found Radha looking at him with the light of love in her eyes. After that there had been a few brief and furtive meetings when the unlettered but romantic youth had declared his love in passionate though halting words. But his parents had killed both ambitions. Circus work was too lowly and immoral for a respectable peasant. Anyway, his father, grandfather and all his ancestors had tilled the land, so he too had to do it. As for marrying Radha, a Hindu, a Kafir, the very idea was infamous and irreligious.

For some time, Rahim Khan, with youthful resentment, toyed with the idea of open rebellion. But the tradition of centuries of serfdom ran in his blood and, however indignant he might have felt at his father's severity, he could not summon enough courage to defy paternal authority and social traditions. After a few days, the circus left the village without Rahim Khan, and the furtive romance with Radha, too, came to an abrupt end. Rahim Khan's father slyly suggested to Ram Charan that his daughter was now fifteen and ought to have been married long ago, not failing to hint at the disastrous consequences of late marriages. Within a few weeks Radha was married to Ram Lal, a middle-aged, pot-bellied banya of the neighbouring village. With a few tears shed in the solitude of the night in memory of her hopeless romance with Rahim Khan, she quickly reconciled herself to her fate and proceeded forthwith to be the mother of half-a-dozen children.

Rahim Khan also married. He had, of course, no choice in the matter. His parents selected the girl, fixed the date, ordered some gaudy clothes for him and some silver ornaments for his bride, sat him on a horse and, to the beat of a brass band, took him to the girl's house where the Nikah was duly performed. To the Kazi's formal questions Rahim Khan mechanically nodded his head. Any other course was impossible. Nobody, of course, cared to ask the shy little girl who sat huddled in a dark room only dimly conscious of the fate to which she had been condemned. After the ceremony, Rahim Khan's father, in a mood of self-congratulation, boasted to his wife; 'See how really he obeyed me. You always feared he might refuse to fall in with our arrangements. I know these youngsters. They are apt to be restless if their marriage is delayed. That is why our fathers believed in marrying away their children early. Now he will be all right!'

At that very moment, standing on the threshold of the room where his wife awaited him much as a sheep awaits the butcher, Rahim Khan made a terrible resolve to avenge himself on his parents, his family, on society. He held them all responsible for the frustration of his life's dreams. And in his confused, illogical mind he regarded his bride as the symbol of the persecution to which he had been subjected. On her he would wreak his vengeance. Iron entered his hitherto kindly soul as he rudely pushed open the door.

That was thirty years ago, Rahim Khan reflected as he lay there on his cot in the dark hut. And hadn't he had his revenge? For thirty years he had ill-treated his wife, his children and his bullocks, quarrelled with everyone in the village and made himself the most hated person in the whole community. The thought of being so universally detested gave him grim satisfaction.

No one in the village, of course, understood or tried to understand the reasons for this strange transformation of the cheerful and kind young man into the beast that he had become. At first, their attitude towards him was one of astonished hostility, but later it changed to indifference mingled with fear of understanding and sympathy he received none. Shunned by everyone, with a bitterness ever gnawing at his heart, Rahim Khan sought consolation in the unquestioned authority over his wife which society allowed him.

For thirty years his wife had submitted to his persecution with the slave-like docility that is the badge of her tribe. Lately, indeed, she had become so used to corporal chastisement that it seemed unnatural if a whole week passed without a beating. To Rahim Khan beating his wife had become a part of his very existence. As sleep gathered round him, his last thought was whether he would be able to endure a life without having an opportunity of indulging in what had now become his second nature. It was perhaps the only moment when Rahim Khan had a feeling, not exactly of affection, for his wife, but of loneliness without her. Never before had he realised how much the woman he hated was a part of his life.

When he awoke it was already late forenoon and he started the day by cursing his wife, for it was she who used to wake him early every morning. But he was in no great hurry today. Lazily he got up and, after his ablutions, milked the goats for his breakfast which consisted of the remains of the previous day's chapattis soaked in the fresh milk. Then he sat down for a smoke, with his beloved hookah beside him. Now the hut was warm and alight with the rays of the sun streaming in through the open window. In a corner they revealed some cobwebs and, having already decided to absent himself from his fields, he thought he would tidy his hut. Tying some rags to the end of the long pole, he was about to remove the cobwebs when he saw a nest in the thatched roof. Two sparrows were fluttering in and out, twittering constantly.

His first impulse was to wreck the nest with one stroke of his pole, but something within him made him desist. Throwing down the pole, he brought a stool and climbed upon it to get a better view of the sparrows' home. Two little featherless mites of red flesh, baby sparrows hardly a day old, lay inside, while their parents hovered round Rahim Khan's face, screaming threateningly. He barely had a glimpse of the inside of the nest when the mother sparrow attacked him.

'Oh damn, you vixen, you might have plucked out my eye,' exclaimed Rahim Khan with his characteristic hollow laugh, and climbed down from his perch. He was strangely amused by the little bird's heroic efforts to save their home and children. The sparrows' nest suffered no harm that day and peace reigned in Rahim Khan's hut.

Next day he resumed his daily work. Still no one talked to him in the village. From morning till late in the afternoon he would toil in the field, ploughing the furrow and watering the crops, but he returned home before sunset. Then he would lie on his cot, smoking his hookah and watching with lively interest the antics of the sparrow family. The two little ones had now grown into fine young birds, and he called them Nuru and Bundu after his lost sons whom he had not seen for several years. The four sparrows were his only friends in the world. His neighbours were still frightened of him and regarded his recent peaceful behaviour with suspicion. They were genuinely astonished that for some time no one had seen him beating his bullocks. Nathee and Chhiddoo themselves were happy and grateful and their bruised bodies had almost healed.

One monsoon evening, when the sky was overcast with threatening clouds, Rahim Khan returned from the fields a little earlier than usual. He found a group of children playing on the road. They ran away as they saw him, and even left their shoes behind in their haste. In vain did Rahim Khan shout, 'Why are you running away? I am not going to beat you.' Meanwhile, it had started drizzling and he hurried homewards to tie up the bullocks before the big downpour came.

Entering his hut, Rahim Khan lighted the earthenware oil lamp and placed some crumbs of bread for the sparrows before he prepared his own dinner. 'O Nuru! O Bundu!' he shouted, but the sparrows did not come out. Anxious to find out what had happened to his friends, he peeped into the nest and found the quartet scared and sitting huddled up within their feathers. At the very spot where the nest lay, the roof was leaking. Rahim Khan took a ladder and went out in the pouring rain to repair the damage. By the time the job was satisfactorily done he was thoroughly drenched. As he sat on the cot, Rahim Khan sneezed but he did not heed the warning and went to sleep. Next morning he awoke with a high fever.

When the villagers did not see him going to the fields for several days they grew anxious and some of them came to see what was the matter. Through a crack in the door they saw him lying on the cot talking, so they thought, to himself: 'O Bundu, O Nuru, who will feed you when I am gone?'

The peasants shook their heads sympathetically. 'Poor fellow,' they said, 'he has gone mad. We will send for his wife to look after him.'

Next morning when Rahim Khan's wife, anxious and weeping, came with her sons, a group of neighbours collected in sympathy. The door was locked from the inside, and, in spite of loud knocking no one opened it. When they broke their way in they found the large and gaunt frame of Rahim lying in the brooding silence of the room, broken only by the flutterings of four sparrows.

New Words

fringed:	adorned as a fringe or border
hilarious:	loud and merry
communal hookah:	hookah shared by all
patel:	the headman of a village
invocation:	prayer
obsequious:	servile, showing too much respect
gruffly:	in a hoarse (gruff) or rough voice
charpoy:	(in India) a common bedstead
slamming:	shutting
out-pourings:	(here) feelings
embittered:	full of bitterness; angry
baniya:	(an Indian) trader
soul-mate:	a companion for his soul. His love was almost spiritual
vanquishing:	defeating
furtive:	secret, stolen, stealthy
kafir:	an unbeliever
resentment:	displeasure and anger. Rahim Khan resented his father's refusal to permit him to marry Radha and to join the circus
toyed with:	played; i.e. he did not actually break out into rebellion
serfdom:	dependence. A serf is a peasant bound to the soil and to his master
paternal authority:	the authority of a father

slyly:	secretly
fall in:	agree
frustration:	failure
iron entered his soul:	he became hard-hearted
shunned:	avoided
gnawing:	biting
docility:	passive obedience
the badge of her tribe:	the characteristic of all wives
corporal:	physical
chastisement:	punishment
second nature:	acquired habit
ablutions:	washing of the body or part of it, as part of a religious rite
vixen:	a female fox; (here) an ill-tempered woman
antics:	ludicrous action
overcast:	clouded over
quartet:	group of four (birds)

Comprehension

1. Can you say what Rahim Khan's occupation was? How do you know? How old was he?
2. What words and expressions are used in paragraph 1 to describe Rahim Khan?
3. How was Rahim Khan's nature reflected in the kind of hut he lived in (paragraph 2)? On entering his house, what information did he receive? What do *you* think—had Rahim Khan's wife run away or was she visiting her brother?
4. When Rahim Khan heard that his wife had gone away, what was his first reaction? Relief? Unhappiness? Anger? Why was he angry on hearing the news? How long was he married? How had he looked upon his wife—as someone loving and valuable or as 'a necessary piece of furniture'?

5. Rahim Khan had two ambitions when he was young—what were they? What were his parents' objections to his joining the circus and his desire to marry Radha? Was he a rebel? Did he defy paternal authority and social traditions when his wishes were turned down?
6. How long did Radha suffer when her romance with Rahim Khan failed? What happened to the latter soon after? Was his meek, submissive behaviour (at the time of his wedding) real or deceptive? Why do you think so?
7. Who did Rahim Khan hold responsible for the frustration of his dreams? Who became the symbol of the persecution he had experienced? Did he succeed in wreaking his vengeance on society? How did he avenge himself? Something had become his second nature—what was it?
8. What influence did the nest have on him? How did the sparrows affect his usual violent conduct? Why were the villagers suspicious of his recent peaceful behaviour?
9. How did Rahim Khan get drenched? What does this act show about his relationship with the sparrows? What was his only worry during the last moments?
10. Why had Rahim Khan's sons run away? When did they return home? Would Rahim Khan have liked to see them? Was he able to do so?

Steps to Interpretation

1. '. . . .he walked. . . . . .with a haughty and unfriendly air'—What does this suggest about Rahim Khan's reputation in the village? What does the phrase 'cautious whispers' (paragraph 1) suggest about the attitude of the villagers towards Rahim Khan? Is it one of respect, or of fear, or a mixture of both?
2. According to the village patel, Rahim Khan had compassion neither for children nor for helpless animals. How was this reflected in his actions? Do you think his actions were justified at least on some occasions?

3. Something made Rahim Khan desist from wrecking the sparrows' nest when he first noticed it. What do you think it was?
4. Can you suggest how Rahim Khan must have felt when the group of children ran away on seeing him?
5. What does Rahim Khan's behaviour towards the sparrows show about his own nature? Is his transformation into a cruel man and then again into a kind man convincing? Do you agree that Rahim Khan is actually portrayed as a likeable figure? How does the author secure the reader's sympathy for the hero?

The Mother of a Traitor

Maxim Gorky

Maxim Gorky (1868–1936) was the pen-name of Alexei Maximovich Peshkov, the great central figure in modern Russian literature. He was born in an artisan family in Nizhny Novgorod, a city now renamed after him. After a miserable childhood in his grandfather's house —his father had died when he was very young— Gorky wandered about like a tramp for several years, enduring misery and poverty, but mixing with the downtrodden who later peopled his stories and novels.

Gorky began writing in 1892. His first works were mainly romantic stories; he later graduated to Chekovian-type stories of dreary lives and useless intellectuals. With his increasing involvement in Bolshevism and the Revolution, his novels became artistic exposures of the evils of capitalistic society. After the Revolution, Gorky had immense influence on the progress of literature and the arts in Soviet Russia. In the last years of his life he was appointed Head of the Soviet Writers' Union, and founded the School of Soviet Realism.

Among the best-known of Gorky's works are: *The Mother*, the first comprehensive portrait of the Russian socialist movement, *Childhood*, *Among the People* and *My Universities*, the autobiographical trilogy, and *The Lower Depths*, a play which was a great success in Russia and was produced all over Europe.

One can talk endlessly about Mothers. For several weeks enemy hosts had surrounded the city in a tight ring of steel; by night fires were lit and the flames peered through the inky blackness at the walls of the city like a myriad red eyes—they blazed malevolently, and their menacing glare evoked gloomy thoughts within the beleaguered city.

From the walls they saw the enemy noose draw tighter; saw the dark shadows hovering about the fires, and heard the neighing of well-fed horses, the clanging of weapons, the loud laughter and singing of man confident of victory—and what can be more jarring to the ear than the songs and laughter of the enemy?

The enemy had thrown corpses into all the streams that fed water to the city, they had burned down the vineyards around the walls, trampled the fields, cut down the orchards—the city was now exposed on all sides, and nearly every day the cannon and muskets of the enemy showered it with lead and iron.

Detachments of war-weary, half-starved soldiers trooped sullenly through the narrow streets of the city; from the windows of houses issued the groans of the wounded, the cries of the delirious, the prayers of women and the wailing of children. People spoke in whispers, breaking off in the middle of a sentence, tensely alert; was not that the enemy advancing?

Worst of all were the nights; in the nocturnal stillness the groans and cries were more distinctly audible; black shadows crept stealthily from the gorges of the distant mountains towards the half-demolished walls, hiding the enemy camp from view, and over the black ridges of the mountains rose the moon like a lost shield dented by sword blows.

And the people in the city, despairing of succour, worn out by toil and hunger, their hope of salvation waning from day to day, the people in the city stared in horror at that moon, at the sharp-toothed ridges of the mountains, the black mass of the gorges and the noisy camp of the enemy. Everything spoke to them of death, and not a star was there in the sky to give them consolation.

They were afraid to light the lamps in the houses, and a heavy darkness enveloped the streets, and in this darkness, like a fish stirring in the depths of a river, a woman draped from head to foot in a black cloak moved soundlessly.

When they saw her, people whispered to one another:

'Is it she?'

'It is she!'

And they withdrew into the niches under archways, or hurried past her with lowered heads. The patrol chiefs warned her sternly:

'Abroad again, Monna Marianna? Take care, you may be killed and nobody will bother to search for the culprit. . .'

She drew herself up and stood waiting, but the patrols passed by, either not daring or else scorning to raise their hand against her; the armed men avoided her like a corpse and, left alone in the darkness, she continued her solitary wanderings from street to street, soundless and black like the incarnation of the city's misfortune, while all about her, as though pursuing her, melancholy sounds issued from the night; the groans, cries, prayers and the sullen murmur of soldiers who had lost all hope of victory.

A citizen and a mother, she thought of her son and her country: for at the head of the men who were destroying her town was her son, her gay, handsome, heartless son. Yet, not so long ago she had looked upon him with pride regarding him as her precious gift to her country, a beneficient force she had brought forth to aid the people of the city where she herself had been born and reared. Her heart was bound by hundreds of invisible threads to these ancient stones with which her forefathers had built their homes and raised the walls of the city; to the soil wherein lay buried the bones of her kinsfolk, to the legends, the songs and the hopes of the people. And now this heart had lost a loved one and it wept. She weighed in her heart as on scales her love for her son and her love for her native city, and she could not tell which weighed the more.

And so she wandered thus by night through the streets, and many, failing to recognise her, drew back in fear, mistaking her black figure for the incarnation of Death that was so near to all of them, and when they did recognise her, they turned silently away from the mother of a traitor.

But one day in a remote corner by the city walls she saw another woman, kneeling beside a corpse, so still that she seemed part of the earth. The woman was praying, her grief-stricken face upturned to the stars. And on the wall overhead the sentries spoke in low tones, their weapons grating against the stone.

The traitor's mother asked:

'Your husband?'

'No.'

'Your brother?'

'My son. My husband was killed thirteen days ago. my son today.'

And rising from her knees, the mother of the slain man said humbly:

'The Madonna sees all and knows all, and I am grateful to her!'

'For what?' asked the first, and the other replied:

'Now that he has died honourably fighting for his country I can say that I feared for him: he was light-hearted, too fond of revelry and I feared that he might betray his city, as did the son of Marianna, the enemy of God and Man, the leader of our foes, may he be so cursed and the womb that bore him!'

Marianna covered her face and went on her way. The next morning she appeared before the city's defenders and said:

'My son has come to be your enemy. Either kill me or open the gates that I may go to him. . .'

They replied:

'You are a human being, and your country must be precious to you; your son is as much an enemy to you as to each one of us.'

'I am his mother. I love him and feel that I am to blame for what he has become!'

Then they took counsel with one another and decided:

'It would not be honourable to kill you for the sins of your son. We know that you could not have led him to commit this terrible sin, and we can understand your distress. But the city does not need you even as a hostage; your son cares nought for you, we believe that he has forgotten you, fiend that he is, and there is your punishment if you think you have deserved it! We believe that is more terrible than death itself!'

'Yes,' she said. 'It is indeed more terrible.'

And so they opened the gates and suffered her to leave the city and watched long from the battlements as she departed from her native soil, now drenched with the blood her son had spilt. She walked slowly, for her feet were reluctant to tear themselves away from this soil, and she bowed to the corpses of the city's defenders, kicking aside a broken weapon in disgust, for all weapons are abhorrent to mothers save those that protect life.

She walked as though she carried a precious phial of

water beneath her cloak and feared to spill a drop and as her figure grew smaller and smaller to those who watched from the city wall, it seemed to them that with her went their dejection and hopelessness.

They saw her pause halfway and throwing back the hood of her cloak turn back and gaze long at the city. And over in the enemy's camp they saw her alone in the field and figures dark as her own approached her cautiously. They approached and inquired who she was and whence she had come.

'Your leader is my son,' she said, and not one of the soldiers doubted it. They fell in beside her, singing his praises, saying how clever and brave he was, and she listened to them with head proudly raised, showing no surprise, for her son could not be otherwise.

And now, at last, she stood before him whom she had known nine months before his birth, him whom she had never felt apart from her own heart. In silk and velvet he stood before her, his weapons studded with precious stones. All was as it should be, thus had she seen him so many times in her dreams—rich, famous and admired.

'Mother!' he said, kissing her hands. 'Thou hast come to me, thou art with me, and tomorrow I shall capture that accursed city!'

'The city where thou wert born,' she reminded him.

Intoxicated with his prowess, crazed with the thirst for more glory, he answered her with the arrogant heat of youth:

'I was born into the world and for the world, and I mean to make the world quake with wonder of me! I have spared this city for thy sake, it has been like a thorn in my flesh and has retarded my swift rise to fame. But now tomorrow I shall smash that nest of obstinate fools!'

'Where every stone knows and remembers them as a child,' she said.

'Stones are dumb unless man makes them speak. Let the mountains speak of me, that is what I wish!'

'And what of men?' she asked.

'Ah yes, I have not forgotten them, Mother. I need them too, for only in men's memory are heroes immortal!'

She said: 'A hero is he who creates life in defiance of death, who conquers death. . . . .'

'No!' he objected. 'The destroyer is as glorious as the builder of a city. See, we do not know who it was that built Rome—Aeneas or Romulus—yet we know well the name of Alaric and the other heroes who destroyed the city. . .'

'Which outlived all names,' the mother reminded him.

Thus they conversed until the sun sank to rest; less and less frequently did she interrupt his wild speech, lower sank her proud head.

A Mother creates, she protects, and to speak to her of destruction means to speak against her; but he did not know this, he did not know that he was negating her reason for existence.

A Mother is always opposed to death; the hand that brings death into the house of men, is hateful and abhorrent to Mothers. But the son did not perceive this, for he was blinded by the cold glitter of glory that deadens the heart.

Nor did he know that a Mother can be as clever and ruthless as she is fearless, when the life she creates and cherishes is in question.

She sat with bowed head, and through the opening in the leader's richly appointed tent she saw the city where first she had felt the sweet tremor of life within her and the anguished convulsions of the birth of this child who now thirsted for destruction.

The crimson rays of the sun dyed the walls and towers of the city blood-red, cast a baleful glare on the windowpanes so that the whole city seemed to be a mass of wounds with the crimson sap of life flowing from each gash. Presently the city turned black as a corpse and the stars shone above it like funeral candles.

She saw the dark houses where people feared to light candles so as not to attract the attention of the enemy, saw the streets steeped in gloom and rank with the stench of corpses, heard the muffled whispers of people awaiting death—she saw it all, all that was near and dear to her stood before her, dumbly awaiting her decision, and she felt herself the mother of all those people in her city.

Clouds descended from the black peaks into the valley and swooped down like winged steeds upon the doomed city.

'We may attack tonight,' said her son, 'if the night is dark enough! It is hard to kill when the sun shines in your eyes and the glitter of the weapons blinds you, many a blow goes awry,' he remarked, examining his sword.

The mother said to him: 'Come, my son, lay thy head on my breast and rest, remember how gay and kind thou wert as a child, and how everyone loved thee. . .'

He obeyed her, laid his head in her lap and closed his eyes, saying:

'I love only glory and I love thee for having made me as I am.'

'And women?' she asked bending over him.

'They are many, one tires of them as of everything that is too sweet.'

'And dost thou not desire children?' she asked finally.

'What for? That they might be killed? Someone like me will kill them; that will give me pain and I shall be too old and feeble to avenge them.'

'Thou art handsome, but as barren as a streak of lightning,' she said with a sigh.

'Yes, like lightning. . .' he replied, smiling.

And he dozed there on his mother's breast like a child.

Then, covering him with her black cloak, she plunged a knife into his heart, and with a shudder he died, for who knew better then she where her son's heart beat. And, throwing his corpse at the feet of the astonished sentries, she said addressing the city:

'As a Citizen, I have done for my country all I could: as a Mother I remain with my son! It is too late for me to bear another, my life is of no use to anyone.'

And the knife, still warm with his blood, her blood, she plunged with a firm hand into her own breast, and again she struck true, for an aching heart is not hard to find.

New Words

host:	a large number, (here) army
myriad:	a very large number
malevolent:	spiteful, wishing to cause suffering to others
beleaguered:	besieged; surrounded with armed forces
nocturnal:	of the night
gorge:	narrow opening (between mountains)
succour:	help given in time of danger
Madonna:	Mary, mother of Jesus Christ
suffered her:	allowed her
abhorrent:	hateful, disgusting

richly
  appointed: well-equipped and furnished
tremor: shaking, movement
baleful: evil, harmful
go awry: go wrong

Comprehension

1. How were the enemy trying to make the people in the city miserable? In contrast how did the attackers themselves live?
2. 'Is it she?' 'It is she!' What does this exchange tell us about what the people thought of her? What did they do when they saw her? Why?
3. What did the patrol chiefs warn her about? Why would nobody bother to search for the culprit? What did she stand waiting for? Why didn't anything happen?
4. How deep was her attachment to the city? What did she 'weigh in her heart as on scales'? What weighed more? How do we know?
5. Whom did she meet one day in a remote corner by the city walls? What was the slain man's mother proud of? What did the woman say about her? How did this meeting affect her?
6. What did she ask the city's defenders to do? Why did they not oblige her? Why didn't they need her even as a hostage? What according to them was her punishment?
7. How did the enemy soldiers greet her? Did she feel proud? What was she proud of?
8. Why did the son decide to capture the city the same night? Why had he spared it so long? How did she try to dissuade him from his plan?
9. '. . . . . . .She saw it all, all that was near and dear to her stood before her dumbly awaiting her decision. . . . .' What did she decide? Had she decided on this action as she left the city? Or had she hoped she would be able to persuade her son?
10. Why did she kill herself?

Steps to Interpretation

1. The story is a study of a mother. What is the painful conflict in her mind? How does she resolve it? Does she fail as a mother or as a citizen? Or does she succeed as both?
2. 'In silk and velvet he stood before her, his weapons studded with precious stones.' This clearly shows the man's vanity. What other traits of his character are brought out in the story? What were his views on glory, women, and children?
3. There are numerous passages in the story about motherhood. List a few of them.
4. Paragraph 2 is a vivid description of the city surrounded by the enemy. The story is full of such descriptions. Could you pick out a few and discuss how effective they are?
5. '. . . .over the black ridges of the mountains rose the moon like a lost shield dented by sword blows.' There are a number of images drawn from nature throughout the story. ('. . . . .and in this darkness like a fish stirring in the depths of a river, a woman . . . . .moved soundlessly.') Choose a few of them and discuss their beauty and aptness.

The Verger

W. Somerset Maugham

William Somerset Maugham (1874–1965) was educated at Canterbury and Heidelberg. He qualified for the medical profession, but gave up the idea of becoming a doctor after the success of his first novel in 1897. He soon established his reputation as a novelist, short-story writer and playwright. The best-known among his novels are *Of Human Bondage* (1915) which is semi-autobiographical in nature, *The Moon and Sixpence* (1919) which is the fictionalised life of a painter, and *The Razor's Edge* (1944), the story of a young man's search for God and belief.

In most of his stories Maugham appears as a cynic amused at the follies of his fellow men, even though compassion for human weakness is not lacking in them. In *The Verger*, a story taken from a collection called *Cosmopolitans*, he holds up to ridicule one of modern man's most cherished institutions: education.

There had been a christening that afternoon at St. Peter's, Neville Square, and Albert Edward Foreman still wore his verger's gown. He kept his new one, its folds as full and stiff as though it were made not of alpaca but of perennial bronze, for funerals and weddings (St. Peter's, Neville Square, was a church much favoured by the fashionable for these ceremonies) and now he wore only his second best. He wore it with complacence, for it was the dignified symbol of his office, and without it (when he took it off to go home) he had the disconcerting sensation of being somewhat insufficiently clad. He took pains with it; he pressed it and ironed it himself.

During the sixteen years he had been verger of this church he had had a succession of such gowns, but he had never been able to throw them away when they were worn out, and the complete series, neatly wrapped up in brown paper, lay in the bottom drawer of the wardrobe in his bedroom.

The verger busied himself quietly, replacing the painted wooden cover on the marble font, taking away a chair that had been brought for an infirm old lady, and waited for the vicar to have finished in the vestry so that he could tidy up in there and go home. Presently he saw him walk across the chancel, genuflect in front of the high altar and come down the aisle; but he still wore his cassock.

'What's he 'anging about for?' the verger said to himself. 'Don't 'e know I want my tea?'

The vicar had been but recently appointed, a red-faced energetic man in the early forties, and Albert Edward still regretted his predecessor, a clergyman of the old school who preached leisurely sermons in a silvery voice and dined out a great deal with his more aristocratic parishioners. He liked things in church to be just so, but he never fussed; he was not like this new man who wanted to have his finger in every pie. But Albert Edward was tolerant. St. Peter's was in a very good neighbourhood and the parishioners were a very nice class of people. The new vicar had come from the East End and he couldn't be expected to fall in all at once with the discreet ways of his fashionable congregation.

'All this 'ustle,' said Albert Edward. 'But give 'im time, 'e'll learn.'

When the vicar had walked down the aisle so far that he could address the verger without raising his voice more than was becoming in a place of worship he stopped.

'Foreman, will you come into the vestry for a minute? I have something to say to you.'

'Very good, sir.'

The vicar waited for him to come up and they walked up the church together.

'A very nice christening, I thought, sir. Funny 'ow the baby stopped cryin' the moment you took him.'

'I've noticed they very often do,' said the vicar, with a little smile. 'After all I've had a good deal of practice with them.'

It was a source of subdued pride to him that he could nearly always quiet a whimpering infant by the manner in which he held it, and he was not unconscious of the amused admiration with which mothers and nurses watched him settle the baby in the crook of his surpliced arm. The verger knew that it pleased him to be complimented on his talent.

The vicar preceded Albert Edward into the vestry. Albert Edward was a trifle surprised to find the two church-wardens there. He had not seen them come in. They gave him pleasant nods.

'Good afternoon, my lord. Good afternoon sir,' he said to one after the other.

They were elderly men, both of them, and they had been church-wardens almost as long as Albert Eward had been verger. They were sitting now at a handsome refectory table that the old vicar had brought many years before from Italy and the vicar sat down in the vacant chair between them. Albert Edward faced them, the table between him and them, and wondered with slight uneasiness what was the matter. He remembered still the occasion on which the organist had got into trouble and the bother they had all had to hush things up.

In a church like St. Peter's, Neville Square, they couldn't afford a scandal. On the vicar's red face was a look of resolute benignity, but the others bore an expression that was slightly troubled.

'He's been naggin' them, he 'as,' said the verger to himself. 'He's jockeyed them into doin' something, but they don't 'alf like it. That's what it is, you mark my words.'

But his thoughts did not appear on Albert Edward's clean-cut and distinguished features. He stood in a respectful but not obsequious attitude. He had been in service before he was appointed to his ecclesiastical office, but only in very good houses, and his deportment was irreproachable. Starting as a page-boy in the household of a merchant-prince, he had risen by due degrees from the position of fourth to first footman, for a year he had been single-handed butler to a widowed peeress and till the vacancy occurred at St. Peter's, butler with two men under him in the house of a retired ambassador. He was tall, spare, grave and dignified. He looked, if not like a duke, at least like an actor of the old school who specialised in dukes' parts. He had tact, firmness, and self-assurance. His character was unimpeachable.

The vicar began briskly.

'Foreman, we've got something rather unpleasant to say to you. You've been here a great many years and I think his lordship and the general agree with me that you've fulfilled the duties of your office to the satisfaction of everybody concerned.'

The two church-wardens nodded.

'But a most extraordinary circumstance came to my knowledge the other day and I felt it my duty to impart it to the church-wardens. I discovered to my astonishment that you could neither read nor write.'

The verger's face betrayed no sign of embarrassment.

'The last vicar knew that, sir,' he replied. 'He said it didn't make no difference. He always said there was a great deal too much education in the world for 'is taste.'

'It's the most amazing thing I ever heard,' cried the general. 'Do you mean to say that you've been verger of this church for sixteen years and never learned to read or write?'

'I went into service when I was twelve, sir. The cook in the first place tried to teach me once, but I didn't seem to have the knack for it, and then what with one thing and another I never seemed to 'ave the time. I've never really found the want of it. I think a lot of these young fellows waste a rare lot of time reading when they might be doing something useful.'

'But don't you want to know the news?' said the other church-warden. 'Don't you ever want to write a letter?'

'No, me lord, I seem to manage very well without. And of late years now they've all these pictures in the papers I get to know what's goin' on pretty well. His wife's quite a scholar and if I want to write a letter she writes it for me. It's not as if I was a bettin' man.'

The two church-wardens gave the vicar a troubled glance and then looked down at the table.

'Well, Foreman, I've talked the matter over with these gentlemen and they quite agree with that the situation is impossible. At a church like St. Peter's, Neville Square, we cannot have a verger who can neither read nor write.'

Albert Edward's thin, sallow face reddened and he moved uneasily on his feet, but he made no reply.

'Understand me, Foreman, I have no complaint to make against you. You do your work quite satisfactorily; I have the highest opinion both of your character and of your capacity; but we haven't the right to take the risk of some accident that might happen owing to your lamentable ignorance. It's a matter of prudence as well as of principle.'

'But couldn't you learn, Foreman?' asked the general.

'No, sir, I'm afraid I couldn't now. You see I'm not as young as I was and if I couldn't seem able to get the letters in me 'ead when I was a nipper I don't think there's much chance of it now.'

'We don't want to be harsh with you, Foreman,' said the vicar. 'But the church-wardens and I have quite made up our minds. We'll give you three months and if at the end of that time you cannot read and write I'm afraid you'll have to go.'

Albert Edward had never liked the new vicar. He'd said from the beginning that they'd made a mistake when they gave him St. Peter's. He wasn't the type of man they wanted with a classy congregation like that. And now he straightened himself a little. He knew his value and he wasn't going to allow himself to be put upon.

'I'm very sorry, sir, I'm, afraid it's no good. I'm too old a dog to learn new tricks. I've lived a good many years without knowin' 'ow to read and write and without wishin' to praise myself, self-praise is no recommendation. I don't mind sayin' I've done my duty in that state of life in which it 'as pleased a merciful providence to place me, and if I could learn now I don't know as I'd want to.'

'In that case, Foreman, I'm afraid you must go.'

'Yes, sir, I quite understand. I shall be 'appy to 'and in my resignation as soon as you've found somebody to take my place.'

But when Albert Edward with his usual politeness had closed the church door behind the vicar and the two church-wardens he could not sustain the air of unruffled dignity with which he had borne the blow inflicted upon him and his lips quivered. He walked slowly back to the vestry and hung up on its proper peg his verger's gown. He sighed as he thought of all the grand funerals and smart weddings it had seen. He tidied everything up, put on his coat, and hat in hand walked down the aisle. He locked the church door behind him. He strolled across the square, but deep in his sad thoughts he did not take the street that led him home, where a nice strong cup of tea awaited him; he took the wrong turning. He walked slowly along. His heart was heavy. He did not know what he should do with himself. He did not fancy the notion of going back to domestic service; after being his own master for so many years, for the vicar and church-wardens could say what they liked, it was he that had run St. Peter's, Neville Square, he could scarcely demean himself by accepting a situation. He had saved a tidy sum, but not enough to live on without doing something, and life seemed to cost more every year. He had never thought to be troubled with such questions. The vergers of St. Peter's, like the popes of Rome, were there for life. He had often thought of the pleasant reference the vicar would make in his sermon at evensong the first Sunday after his death to the long and faithful service and the exemplary character of their late verger, Albert Edward Foreman. He sighed deeply. Albert Edward was a non-smoker and a total abstainer, but with a certain latitude; that is to say, he liked a glass of beer with his dinner and when he was tired he enjoyed a cigarette. It occurred to him now that one would comfort him, and since he did not carry them he looked about him for a shop where he could buy a packet of Gold Flakes. He did not at once see one and walked on a little. It was a long street, with all sorts of shops in it, but there was not a single one where you could buy cigarettes.

'That's strange,' said Albert Edward.

To make sure, he walked right up the street again. No, there was no doubt about it. He stopped and looked reflectively up and down.

'I can't be the only man as walks along this street and wants a fag,' he said. 'I shouldn't wonder but what a fellow might do very well with a little shop here. Tobacco and sweets you know.'

He gave a sudden start.

'That's an idea,' he said. 'Strange 'ow things come to you when you least expect it.'

He turned, walked home, and had his tea.

'You're very silent this afternoon, Albert,' his wife remarked.

'I'm thinkin',' he said.

He considered the matter from every point of view and next day he went along the street and by good luck found a little shop to let that looked as though it would exactly suit him. Twenty-four hours later he had taken it, and when a month after that he left St. Peter's, Neville Square, for ever, Albert Edward Foreman set up in business as a tobacconist and news agent. His wife said it was a dreadful come-down after being verger of St. Peter's, but he answered that you had to move with the times, the church wasn't what it was, and 'enceforward he was going to render unto Caesar what was Caesar's. Albert Edward did very well. He did so well that in a year or so it struck him that he might take a second shop and put a manager in. He looked for another long street that hadn't got a tobacconist in it and when he found it, and a shop to let, took it and stocked it. This was a success too. Then it occurred to him that if he could run two he could run half a dozen, so he began walking about London, and whenever he found a long street that had no tobacconist and a shop to let he took it. In the course of ten years he had acquired no less than ten shops and he was making money hand over fist. He went round to all of them himself every Monday, collected the week's takings, and took them to the bank.

One morning when he was there paying in a bundle of notes and a heavy bag of silver the cashier told him that the manager would like to see him. He was shown into an office and the manager shook hands with him.

'Mr Foreman, I wanted to have a talk with you about the money you've got on deposit with us. D'you know exactly how much it is?'

'Not within a pound or two, sir; but I've got a pretty rough idea.'

'Apart from what you paid in this morning it's a little over thirty thousand pounds. That's a very large sum to have on deposit and I should have thought you'd do better to invest it.'

'I wouldn't want to take no risk, sir. I know it's safe in the bank.'

'You needn't have the least anxiety. We'll make you out a list of absolutely gilt-edged securities. They'll bring you in a better rate of interest than we can possibly afford to give you.'

A troubled look settled on Mr Foreman's distinguished face. 'I've never 'ad anything to do with stocks and shares and I'd 'ave to leave it all in your 'ands,' he said.

The manager smiled. 'We'll do everything. All you'll have to do next time you come in is just to sign the transfers.'

'I could do that all right,' said Albert uncertainly. 'But 'ow should I know what I was signin'?'

'I suppose you can read,' said the manager a trifle sharply.

Mr Foreman gave him a disarming smile.

'Well, sir, that's just it. I can't. I know it sounds funny like, but there it is, I can't read or write, only me name, an' I only learnt to do that when I went into business.'

The manager was so surprised that he jumped up from his chair.

'That's the most extraordinary thing I ever heard.'

'You see, it's like this, sir, I never 'ad the opportunity until it was too late and then some'ow I wouldn't. I got obstinate like.'

The manager stared at him as though he were a prehistoric monster.

'And do you mean to say that you've built up this important business and amassed a fortune of thirty thousand pounds without being able to read or write? Good God, man, what would you be now if you had been able to?'

'I can tell you that, sir,' said Mr Foreman, a little smile on his still aristocratic features. 'I'd be verger of St. Peter's, Neville Square.'

New Words

verger:	attendant in a church
complacence:	self-satisfaction
disconcerting:	upsetting
font:	a stone basin to hold holy water in a church
vestry:	rooms in a church where the priest puts on his robes for religious ceremonies
chancel:	part of the church where the altar stands
genuflect:	kneel in prayer
cassock:	gown worn by a priest when he performs religious ceremonies in the church

'anging about: (hanging about) staying on
regretted his predecessor: felt sorry that the previous vicar had left
(has) his finger in every pie: interfered in every matter
congregation: people who take part in religious worship
'ustle: (hustle), noisy activity
surplice: loose gown with wide sleeves worn over a cassock during church services
churchwardens: elected representatives of the people worshipping in a church, they help in the administration
refectory: dining hall
resolute benignity: firm but kind manner
nagging: worrying
jockeyed: (here) forced
footman: servant who admits visitors
unimpeachable: that which cannot be questioned or doubted
nipper: (colloquial) small child
classy: aristocratic
evensong: evening prayers at church
latitude: flexibility
fag: cigarette
come-down: lowering of status
render unto Ceasar what was Ceasar's: (a quotation from the Bible) hereaftereh would attend to his own affairs
hand over fist steadily and rapidly
gilt-edged securities: shares or any other form of investment hich is/are absolutely safe.

Comprehension

1. In what ways was the new vicar of St. Peter's different from the old one? How did these differences change the course of the story?
2. What was the young vicar proud of? Was Foreman trying to flatter him when he complimented the vicar on this?
3. What had the vicar 'jockeyed' the churchwardens into doing? Did they like doing it? What was the vicar's reasons for his action?
4. How did Foreman receive the vicar's announcement? Did he take long to make up his mind? How did he feel later?
5. Walking out of the church, deep in his sad thoughts, Foreman took the wrong turning. How did this mistake change his life?
6. How strict a non-smoker and non-drinker was Foreman? What did he look for in the street? Did he find one? What did this search result in?
7. 'You are very silent this afternoon, Albert,' said his wife. 'I'm thinkin',' he said. What was he thinking about? Did he act soon? How did his business grow into a big one?
8. What was the bank manager's proposition? Did Foreman like it? Why did he look troubled? How did the manager reassure him?
9. 'I suppose you can read,' said the manager a trifle sharply. Why did he speak sharply? What did he think Foreman was doing?
10. What was the surprised bank manager's final question? What was Mr Foreman's answer?

Steps to Interpretation

1. Foreman wore his verger's gown with complacence. He liked being a verger. Indeed, he was proud of

being one. What other words and actions of his show you he loved his job?

2. You see the new vicar of St. Peter's mostly through the eyes of Foreman. What kind of picture do you get of him through Foreman? Do you think it is distorted because Foreman is prejudiced against him?

3. We are told that Foreman was 'tall, spare, grave, and dignified'. What other descriptions of physical appearance and traits of character do you get in the story? How are these traits exemplified through his actions and decisions?

4. 'Don't 'e know I want my tea?' the verger said to himself. In 'educated English' it should be 'Doesn't he know. . . .?' (Not surprising, for the man did not know how to read and write.) Can you spot a few more examples of the same kind and render them into 'acceptable' English?

5. In this story Maugham is trying to laugh at some ridiculous features of English social life, reflected in the congregation of St. Peter's, its vicar, churchwardens and its verger. Mention a few of them.

6. Foreman, an uneducated man, amasses a large fortune. Is education necessary for financial success? How do you think education helps a person?

7. Is a man who can read and write 'educated'? At what aspect of 'education' is Maugham laughing?

Kong Yiji

Lu Xun

Lu Xun (1881–1936) is the pen-name of Zhou Shuren, one of the most reputed writers of modern China. Born in Shaoxing, he studied in a naval academy and then in a school of mining. Later, in the middle of a medical course, he realised that he could be of more use to China as a writer, curing her mental problems, than as a physician.

Lu Xun wrote not to entertain but to shock and enlighten. A scholar of great distinction, he rejected the old culture. In *Kong Yiji* he shows how decrepit the traditional Confucian culture was, a representative and victim of which is the poor scholar in the story.

The layout of Luzhen's taverns is unique. In each, facing you as you enter, is a bar in the shape of a carpenter's square where hot water is kept ready for warming rice wine. When men come off work at midday and in the evening they spend four coppers on a bowl of wine—or so they did twenty years ago; now it costs ten—and drink this warm, standing by the bar, taking it easy. Another copper will buy a plate of salted bamboo shoots or peas flavoured with aniseed to go with the wine, while a dozen will buy a meat dish; but most of the customers here belong to the short-coated class, few of whom can afford this. As for those in long gowns, they go into the inner room to order wine and dishes and sit drinking at their leisure.

At the age of twelve I started work as a pot-boy in the Prosperity Tavern at the edge of the town. The boss put me to work in the outer room, saying that I looked too much of a fool to serve long-gowned customers. The short-coated customers there were easier to deal with, it is true, but among them were quite a few pernickety ones who insisted on watching for themselves while the yellow wine was ladled from the keg, looked for water at the bottom of the wine-pot, and personally inspected the pot's immersion into the hot water. Under such strict surveillance, diluting the wine was very hard indeed. Thus it did not take my boss many days to decide that this job too was beyond me. Luckily I had been recommended by somebody influential, so he could not sack me. Instead I was transferred to the dull task of simply warming wine.

After that I stood all day behind the bar attending to my duties. Although I gave a satisfaction at this post, I found it somewhat boring and monotonous. Our boss was a grim-faced man, nor were the customers much pleasanter, which made the atmosphere a gloomy one. The only times when there was any laughter were when Kong Yiji came to the tavern. That is why I remember him.

Kong Yiji was the only long-gowned customer who used to drink his wine standing. A big, pallid man whose wrinkled face often bore scars, he had a large, unkempt, and grizzled beard. And although he wore a long gown, it was dirty and tattered. It had not, by the look of it, been washed or mended for ten years or more. He used so many archaisms in his speech that half of it was barely intelligible. And as his surname was Kong, he was given the nickname Kong Yiji, from Kong, Yi, ji, the first three characters in the old-fashioned children's copy-book. Whenever he came in, everyone there would look at him and chuckle. And someone was sure to call out:

'Kong Yiji! What are those fresh scars on your face?'

Ignoring this, he would lay nine coppers on the bar and order two bowls of heated wine with a dish of aniseed-peas. Then someone else would bawl:

'You must have been stealing again!'

'Why sully a man's good name for no reason at all?' Kong Yiji would ask, raising his eyebrows.

'Good name? Why, the day before yesterday you were trussed up and beaten for stealing books from the He family. I saw you!'

At that Kong Yiji would flush, the veins on his forehead standing out as he protested, 'Taking books can't be counted as stealing......Taking books....for a scholar. . .can't be counted as stealing.' Then followed such quotations from the classics as 'A gentleman keeps his integrity even in poverty,' together with a spate of archaisms which soon had everybody roaring with laughter, making the whole tavern ring with their voices.

From the gossip that I heard, it seemed that Kong Yiji had studied the classics but never passed the official examinations and, not knowing any way to make a living, he had grown steadily poorer until he was almost reduced to beggary. Luckily he was a good calligrapher and could find enough copying work to fill his rice-bowl. But unfortunately he had his failings too: laziness and a love of tippling. So after a few days he would disappear, taking with him books, paper, brushes, and inkstone. And after this had happened several times, people stopped employing him as a copyist. Then all he could do was resort to occasional pilfering. In our tavern, though, he was a model customer who never failed to pay up. Sometimes, it is true, when he had no ready money, his name would be chalked up on our tally-board; but in less than a month he invariably settled the bill, and the name Kong Yiji would be wiped off the board again.

After Kong Yiji had drunk half a bowl of wine, his flushed cheeks would stop burning. But then someone would ask:

'Kong Yiji, can you really read?'

When he glanced back as if such a question were not worth answering, they would continue: 'How is it you never passed even the lowest official examination?'

At once a grey tinge would overspread Kong Yiji's dejected, discomfited face, and he would mumble more of those unintelligible archaisms. Then everyone there would laugh heartily again, making the whole tavern ring with their voices.

At such times I could join in the laughter with no danger of a dressing down from my boss. In fact he always put such questions to Kong Yiji himself, to raise a laugh. Knowing that it was no use talking to the men, Kong Yiji would chat with us boys. Once he asked me:

'Have you had any schooling?'

When I nodded curtly he said, 'Well then, I'll test you. How do you write the *hui*[1] in aniseed-peas?'

Who did this beggar think he was, testing me? I turned away and ignored him. After waiting for some time he said earnestly:

'You can't write it, eh? I'll show you. Mind you remember. You ought to remember such characters, because you'll need them to write up your accounts when you have a shop of your own.'

It seemed to me that I was still very far from having a shop of my own; in addition to which, our boss never

[1] A Chinese character meaning 'aniseed'.

entered aniseed-peas in his account book. Half amused and half exasperated, I drawled: 'I don't need you to show me. Isn't it the *hui* written with the element for grass?'

Kong Yiji's face lit up. Tapping two long finger-nails on the bar, he nodded. 'Quite correct!' he said. 'There are four different ways of writing *hui*. Do you know them?'

But my patience exhausted, I scowled and moved away. Kong Yiji had dipped his finger in wine to trace the characters on the bar. When he saw my utter indifference, his face fell and he sighed.

Sometimes children in the neighbourhood, hearing laughter, came in to join in the fun and surrounded Kong Yiji. Then he would give them aniseed-peas, one a piece. After eating the peas the children would still hang round, their eyes fixed on the dish. Growing flustered, he would cover it with his hand and bending forward from the waist would say: 'There aren't many left, not many at all.' Straightening up to look at the peas again, he would shake his head and reiterate: 'Not many, I do assure you. Not many, nay, not many at all.' Then the children would scamper off shouting with laughter.

That was how Kong Yiji contributed to our enjoyment, but we got along all right without him too.

One day, shortly before the Mid-Autumn Festival I think it was, my boss who was slowly making out his accounts took down the tally-board. 'Kong Yiji hasn't shown up for a long time,' he remarked suddenly. 'He still owes nineteen coppers.' That made me realise how long it was since we had seen him.

'How could he?' rejoined one of the customers. 'His legs were broken in that last beating up.'

'Ah!' said my boss.

'He'd been stealing again. This time he was fool enough to steal from Mr Ding, the provincial-grade scholar. As if anybody could get away with that!'

'So what happened?'

'What happened? First he wrote a confession, then he was beaten. The beating lasted nearly all night, and they broke both his legs.'

'And then?'

'Well, his legs were broken.'

'Yes, but after?'

'After?. . .Who knows? He may be dead.'

My boss asked no further questions but went on slowly making up his accounts.

After the Mid-Autumn Festival the wind grew daily colder as winter approached, and even though I spent all my time by the stove I had to wear a padded jacket. One afternoon, when the tavern was deserted, as I sat with my eyes closed I heard the words:

'Warm a bowl of wine.'

It was said in a low but familiar voice. I opened my eyes. There was no one to be seen. I stood up to look out. There below the bar, facing the door, sat Kong Yiji. His face was thin and grimy—he looked a wreck. He had on a ragged lined jacket, and was squatting cross-legged on a mat which was attached to his shoulders by a straw rope. When he saw me he repeated:

'Warm a bowl of wine.'

At this point my boss leaned over the bar to ask: Is that Kong Yiji? You still owe nineteen coppers.'

'That. . .I'll settle next time.' He looked up dejectedly. ' Here's cash. Give me some good wine.'

My boss, just as in the past, chuckled and said:

'Kong Yiji, you've been stealing again!'

But instead of a stout denial, the answer simply was:

' Don't joke with me.'

'Joke? How did your legs get broken if you hadn't been stealing?'

'I fell,' whispered Kong Yiji. 'Broke them in a fall.' His eyes pleaded with the boss to let the matter drop. By now several people had gathered round, and they all laughed with the boss. I warmed the wine, carried it over, and set it on the threshold. He produced four coppers from his ragged coat pocket, and as he placed them in my hand I saw that his own hands were covered with mud—he must have crawled there on them. Presently he finished the wine and, to the accompaniment of taunts and laughter, slowly pushed himself off with his hands.

A long time went by after that without our seeing Kong Yiji again. At the end of the year, when the boss took down the tally-board he said: 'Kong Yiji still owes nineteen coppers.' At the Dragon-Boat Festival the next year he said the same thing again. But when the Mid-Autumn Festival arrived he was silent on the subject, and another New Year came round without our seeing any more of Kong Yiji.

Nor have I ever seen him since—no doubt Kong Yiji really is dead.

New Words

tavern:	public house for the supply of food and drink
pernickety:	fussy; worrying about silly things
surveillance:	close watch
pallid:	pale; ill-looking
archaism:	words or expressions not used now
sully:	stain; discredit
calligrapher:	an expert in beautiful handwriting
tippling:	habit of drinking too much liquor
pilfering:	stealing in small quantities
flustered:	nervous; confused
taunt:	a contemptuous remark

Comprehension

1. How long ago did this story happen? Where is this indicated?
2. What were the two types of customers that Prosperity Tavern entertained? How would you distinguish between them?
3. Why was the atmosphere of the tavern gloomy? Why does the boy remember Kong Yiji?
4. Was Kong Yiji the scholar's real name? How did he get the name? What aspect of his background is made fun of in the name?
5. How did Kong Yiji react to the taunts of people? How did he explain away his stealing books from the He family?
6. How was Kong Yiji reduced to the state in which you find him?
7. How did Kong Yiji try to teach the boy? Why was he disappointed?
8. How did Kong Yiji treat the little boys who surrounded him? What trait of his character is revealed by this?

9. Why didn't Kong Yiji come to the tavern for a long time? What shape was he in when he finally appeared? How did he explain his pitiable state?
10. Did Kong Yiji settle his debt with the tavern? What do you think happened to the old man?

Steps to Interpretation

1. Read the description of the layout of Luzhen's taverns Notice the care with which the author paints the minute details. Are there similar instances of vivid description in the story?
2. The boss thought that the boy was a fool because he was not able to cheat the customers by diluting the wine. What other such improper conduct typical of a decrepit society do you find in the story?
3. What picture of Kong Yiji emerges from the story? Was he a cheat and a thief? Would you sympathise with him?
4. Compare this story with *The Verger*. Is there any point of similarity? Kong Yiji, a scholar, is reduced to petty thieving and he lives a hand-to-mouth existence. Why didn't his education benefit him? Did his education help him at all? In what way?

The Snob

Morley Callaghan

Morley Edward Callaghan (1903–   ) is one of Canada's best known writers. He began writing short stories while he was still a student. Encouraged by Hemingway (who he had met in Paris immediately after World War I) Callaghan published his stories in a wide range of American magazines. A graduate in law—he practised law for a time—most of his stories focus on social outcasts and the conflict between material and moral values.

The Snob is a study of how hidden conflicts affect people's lives and behaviour. Psychologists talk about 'projection'—the impulse to accuse others of traits one cannot admit in oneself. By denouncing these undesirable traits in others, they are trying to relieve their own sense of guilt. Who is the real snob in this story? And who is accused of being one?

It was in the book counter in the department store that John Harcourt, the student, caught a glimpse of his father. At first he could not be sure in the crowd that pushed along the aisle, but there was something about the color of the back of the elderly man's neck, something about the faded felt hat, that he knew very well. Harcourt was standing with the girl he loved, buying a book for her. All afternoon he had been talking to her, eagerly, but with an anxious diffidence, as if there still remained in him an innocent wonder that she should be delighted to be with him. From underneath her wide-brimmed straw hat, her face, so fair and beautifully strong with its expression of cool independence, kept turning up to him and sometimes smiled at what he said. That was the way they always talked, never daring to show much full, strong feeling. Harcourt had just bought the book, and had reached into his pocket for the money with a free, ready gesture to make it appear that he was accustomed to buying books for young ladies, when the white-haired man in the faded felt hat, at the other end of the counter, turned half-toward him, and Harcourt knew he was standing only a few feet away from his father.

The young man's easy words trailed away and his voice became little more than a whisper, as if he were afraid that everyone in the store might recognise it. There was rising in him a dreadful uneasiness; something very precious that he wanted to hold seemed close to destruction. His father, standing at the end of the bargain counter, was planted squarely on his two feet, turning a book over thoughtfully in his hands. Then he took out his glasses from an old, worn leather case and adjusted them on the end of his nose, looking down over them at the book. His coat was thrown open, two buttons on his vest were undone, his hair was too long, in his rather shabby clothes he looked very much like a workingman, a carpenter perhaps. Such a resentment rose in young Harcourt that he wanted to cry out bitterly. 'Why does he dress as if he never owned a decent suit in his life? He doesn't care what the whole world thinks of him. He never did. I've told him a hundred times he ought to wear his good clothes when he goes out. Mother's told him the same thing. He just laughs. And now Grace may see him. Grace will meet him.'

So young Harcourt stood still, with his head down, feeling that something very painful was impeding. Once he looked anxiously at Grace, who had turned to the bargain counter. Among those people drifting aimlessly by, with not red faces, getting in each other's way, using their elbows but keeping their faces detached and wooden, she looked tall and splendidly alone. She was so sure of herself, her relation to the people in the aisles, the clerks behind the counters, the books on the shelves, and everything around her. Still keeping his head down and moving close, he whispered uneasily, 'Let's go and have tea somewhere, Grace.'

'In a minute, dear,' she said.

'Let's go now.'

'In just a minute, dear,' she repeated absently.

'There's not a breath of air in here. Let's go now.'

'What makes you so impatient?'

'There's nothing but old books on that counter.'

'There may be something here I've wanted all my life, she said, smiling at him brightly and not noticing the uneasiness in his face.

So Harcourt had to move slowly behind her, getting closer to his father all the time. He could feel the space that separated them narrowing. Once he looked up with a vague, sidelong glance. But his father, red-faced and happy, was still reading the book, only now there was a meditative expression on his face, as if something in the book had stirred him and he intended to stay there reading for some time.

Old Harcourt had lots of time to amuse himself, because he was on a pension after working hard all his life. He had sent John to the university and he was eager to have him distinguish himself. Every night when John came home, whether it was early or late, he used to go into his father and mother's bedroom and turn on the light and talk to them about the interesting things that had happened to him during the day. They listened and shared this new world with him. They both sat up in their night clothes, and, while his mother asked all the questions, his father listened attentively with his head cocked on one side and a smile or a frown on his face. The memory of all this was in John now, and there was also a desperate longing and a pain within him growing harder to bear as he glanced fearfully at his father, but he thought stubbornly, 'I can't introduce him. It'll be easier for everybody if he doesn't see us. I'm not ashamed. But it will be easier. It'll be more sensible. It'll only embarrass him to see Grace.' By this time he knew he was ashamed, but he felt that his shame was justified, for Grace's father had the smooth, confident manner of a man who had lived all his life among people who were rich and sure of themselves. Often when he had been in Grace's home talking politely to her mother, John had kept on thinking of the plainness of his own home and of his parent's laughing, good-natured untidiness, and he resolved desperately that he must make Grace's people admire him.

He looked up cautiously, for they were about eight feet away from his father, but at that moment his father, too, looked up and John's glance shifted swiftly far over the aisle, over the counters, seeing nothing. As his father's blue, calm eyes stared steadily over the glasses, there was an instant when their glances might have met. Neither one could have been certain, yet John, as he turned away and began to talk hurriedly to Grace, knew surely that his father had seen him. He knew it by the steady calmness in his father's blue eyes. John's shame grew, and then humiliation sickened him as he waited and did nothing.

His father turned away, going down the aisle, walking erectly in his shabby clothes, his shoulders very straight, never once looking back. His father would walk slowly down the street, he knew, with that meditative expression deepening and becoming grave.

Young Harcourt stood beside Grace, brushing against her soft shoulder, and was made faintly aware again of the delicate scent she used. There, so close beside him, she was holding within her everything he wanted to reach out for, only now he felt a sharp hostility that made him sullen and silent.

'You were right, John,' she was drawling in her soft voice. 'It does get unbearable in here on a hot day. Do let's go now. Have you ever noticed that department stores after a time can make you really hate people?' But she smiled when she spoke, so he might see that she really hated no one.

'You don't like people, do you?' he said sharply.

'People? What people? What do you mean?'

'I mean,' he went on irritably, 'you don't like the kind of people you bump into here, for example.'

'Not especially. Who does? What are you talking about?'

'Anybody could see you don't,' he said recklessly, full of a savage eagerness to hurt her. 'I say you don't like simple, honest people, the kind of people you meet all over the city.' He blurted the words out as if he wanted to shake her, but he was longing to say, 'You wouldn't like my family. Why couldn't I take you home to have dinner with them? You'd turn your nose at them, because they've no pretensions. As soon as my father saw you, he knew you wouldn't want to meet him. I could tell by the way he turned.'

His father was on his way home now, he knew, and that evening at dinner they would meet. His mother and sister would talk rapidly, but his father would say nothing to him, or to anyone. There would only be

Harcourt's memory of the level look in the blue eyes, and the knowledge of his father's pain as he walked away.

Grace watched John's gloomy face as they walked through the store, and she knew he was nursing some private rage, and so her own resentment and exasperation kept growing, and she said crisply, ' You're entitled to your moods on a hot afternoon, I suppose, but if I feel I don't like it here, then I don't like it. You wanted to go yourself. Who likes to spend very much time in a department store on a hot afternoon? I begin to hate every stupid person that bangs into me, everybody near me. What does that make me?'

'It makes you a snob.'

'So I'm a snob now?' she asked angrily.

'Certainly you're a snob,' he said. They were at the door going out to the street. As they walked in the sunlight, in the crowd moving slowly down the street, he was groping for words to describe the secret he had always had about her. ' I've always known how you'd feel about people I like who didn't fit into your private world,' he said.

' You're a very stupid person,' she said. Her face was flushed now, and it was hard for her to express her indignation, so she stared straight ahead as she walked along.

They had never talked in this way, and now they were both quickly eager to hurt each other. With a flow of words, she started to argue with him, then she checked herself and said calmly, 'Listen, John, I imagine you're tired of my company. There's no sense in having tea together. I think I'd better leave you right here.'

' That's fine,' he said. 'Good afternoon.'

'Good-bye.'

'Good-bye.'

She started to go, she had gone two paces, but he reached out desperately and held her arm, and he was frightened, and pleading, 'Please don't go, Grace.'

All the anger and irritation had left him; there was just a desperate anxiety in his voice as he pleaded 'Please forgive me. I've no right to talk to you like that. I don't know why I'm so rude or what's the matter. I'm ridiculous. I'm very, very ridiculous. Please, you must forgive me. Don't leave me.'

He had never talked to her so brokenly, and his sincerity, the depth of his feeling, began to stir her. While she listened, feeling all the yearning in him, they seemed to have been brought closer together, by opposing each other, than ever before, and she began to feel almost shy. 'I don't know what's the matter. I suppose we're both irritable. It must be the weather,' she said. But I'm not angry, John.'

He nodded his head miserably. He longed to tell her that he was sure she would have been charming to his father, but he had never felt so wretched in his life. He held her arm tight, as if he must hold it or what he wanted most in the world would slip away from him, yet he kept thinking, as he would ever think, of his father walking away quietly with his head never turning.

New Words

aisle: passage between two rows of seats, shelves etc.

bargain counter: counter at which goods are sold cheap

resentment: feeling that a person has when insulted or humiliated

sure of herself:	self-confident
meditative:	thoughtful
stirred him:	excited him, roused him
hostility:	ill-will
bump into:	knock against
blurt out:	say something suddenly and thoughtlessly
exasperation:	irritation.

Comprehension

1. What was John Harcourt doing in the department store? Who was with him? What were they doing? Was he accustomed to buying books for young ladies?
2. Was John Harcourt sure at first that the elderly man was his father? What made him feel that he was?
3. How was John's father dressed? How did John react to the old man's appearance? Why did he want to go away from the store?
4. Why did John's father have lots of time to amuse himself? Did he have a university education? Was he happy sending John to the university? What daily incident tells us that?
5. Had John met Grace's parents? How does he compare them and their home with his own?
6. Did Old Harcourt see his son? Are we sure? What did John think? How did he know?
7. Did John apologise to Grace? How? What stirred the girl's heart? What had brought them closer together?

Steps to Interpretation

1. John was talking with an *anxious diffidence*. How does his diffidence affect the story? There is a similar phrase in the next sentence which describes the girl's expression. What is it? What caused a *dreadful*

uneasiness in John? What was the 'something precious that seemed close to destruction?

2. 'I can't introduce him. . .' thought John 'I'm not ashamed. . . .' Was that true? What reasons did John give himself for not introducing his father to Grace? What trait of his character does this show?
3. Why did John's shame grow into a sickening humiliation? What told him that his father was deeply hurt? How did this affect John's behaviour to Grace?
4. Why did John feel a sharp hostility towards Grace? What did he accuse her of? Who was the real snob?
5. Did John feel happy after Grace forgave him? Which word tells us he did not? What would always worry him?

On Saturday Afternoon

Alan Sillitoe

In the late 1950's and early 60's there emerged a group of writers with a genuine working class background and concerned with the problems of their class. Alan Sillitoe (1928–) belongs to this eminent group of successful young writers. He was born in Nottingham, left school at the age of fourteen, and after working in a bicycle factory, joined the Royal Air Force as a wireless operator. His first novel, *Saturday Night and Sunday Morning* (1958), was awarded a prize as the best English novel of the year.

In most of his short stories, as in *On Saturday Afternoon*, Sillitoe attempts to demonstrate 'the other side of life', in other words, the working class, the under-educated and under-privileged. This particular story is a poignant tale of a dejected man trying to commit suicide, and told by a sixteen-year-old boy. This story owes its success not only to the appeal of its subject matter but also to the impression it gives of being true to the life with which it deals. Sillitoe obtains this effect by using colloquial, racy language mixed with slang and dialect words and above all, by never attempting to write in a way which would be foreign to his characters.

I once saw a bloke try to kill himself. I'll never forget the day because I was sitting in the house one Saturday afternoon, feeling black and fed-up because everybody in the family had gone to the pictures, except me who'd for some reason been left out of it. 'Course, I didn't know then that I would soon see something you can never see in the same way on the pictures, a real bloke stringing himself up. I was only a kid at the time, so you can imagine how much I enjoyed it.

I've never known a family to look as black as our family when they're fed-up. I've seen the old man with his face so dark and full of murder because he ain't got no fags or was having to use saccharine to sweeten his tea, or even for nothing at all, that I've backed out of the house in case he got up from his fireside chair and came for me. He just sits, almost on top of the fire, his oil-stained Sunday joint maulers opened out in front of him and facing inwards to each other, his thick shoulders scrunched forward, and his dark brown eyes staring into the fire. Now and again he'd say a dirty word, for no reason at all, the worst word you can think of, and when he starts saying this you know it's time to clear out. If mam's in it gets worse than ever, because she says sharp to him: 'What are yo' looking so bloody black for?' as if it might be because of something she's done, and before you know what's happening he's tipped up a tableful of pots and mam's gone out of the house crying. Dad hunches back over the fire and goes on swearing. All because of a packet of fags.

I once saw him broodier than I'd ever seen him, so that I thought he'd gone crackers in a quiet sort of way—until a fly flew to within a yard of him. Then his hand shot out, got it, and slung it crippled into the roaring fire. After that he cheered up a bit and mashed some tea.

Well, that's where the rest of us got our black looks from. It stands to reason we'd have them with a dad who carries on like that, don't it? Black looks run in the family. Some families have them and some don't. Our family has them right enough and that's certain, so when we're fed-up we're really fed-up. Nobody knows why we get as fed-up as we do or why it gives us these black looks when we are. Some people get fed-up and don't look bad at all: They seem happy in a funny sort of way, as if they've just been set free from clink after being in there for something they didn't do, or come out of the pictures after sitting plugged for eight hours at a bad film or just missed a bus they ran half a mile for and seen it was the wrong one just after they'd stopped running—but in our family it's murder for the others if one of us is fed-up. I've asked myself lots of times what it is, but I can never get any sort of answer even if I sit and think for hours, which I must admit I don't do, though it looks good when I say I do. But I sit and think foı long enough, until mam says to me, at seeing me scrunched up over the fire like dad: What are yo' looking so black for?' So I've just got tc stop thinking about it in case I get really black and fed-up and go the same way as dad, tipping up a tableful of pots and all.

Mostly I suppose there's nothing to look so black for: though it's nobody's fault and you can't blame anyone for looking black because I'm sure it's summat in the blood. But on this Saturday afternoon I was looking so black that when dad came in from the bookie's he said to me: 'What's up wi' yo'?'

'I feel badly,' I fibbed. He'd have had a fit if I'd said I was only black because I hadn't gone to the pictures.

'Well, have a wash,' he told me.

'I don't want a wash,' I said, and that was a fact.

'Well, get outside and get some fresh air then,' he shouted.

I did as I was told, double-quick, because if ever dad goes as far as to tell me to get some fresh air I know it's time to get away from him. But outside the air wasn't so fresh, what with that bloody great bike factory bashing away at the yard-end. I didn't know where to go, so I walked up the yard a bit and sat down near somebody's back gate.

Then I saw this bloke who hadn't lived long in our

yard. He was tall and thin and had a face like a parson except that he wore a flat cap and had a moustache that drooped, and looked as though he hadn't had a square meal for a year. I didn't think much o' this at the time: but I remember that as he turned in by the yard-end one of the nosy gossiping women who stood there every minute of the day except when she trudged to the pawn-shop with her husband's bike or best suit, shouted to him: 'What's that rope for, mate?'

He called back: 'It's to 'ang messen wi', missis,' and she cackled at his bloody good joke so loud and long you'd think she never heard such a good 'un though the next day she cackled on the other side of her fat face.

He walked by me puffing a fag and carrying his coil of brand-new rope, and he had to step over me to get past. His boot nearly took my shoulder off, and when I told him to watch where he was going I don't think he heard me because he didn't even look round. Hardly anybody was about. All the kids were still at the pictures, and most of their mams and dads were downtown doing the shopping.

The bloke walked down the yard to his back door, and having nothing better to do because I hadn't gone to the pictures I followed him. You see, he left his back door open a bit, so I gave it a push and went in. I stood there, just watching him, sucking my thumb, the other hand in my pocket. I suppose he knew I was there, because his eyes were moving more natural now, but he didn't seem to mind. 'What are yer going to do wi' that rope, mate?' I asked him.

'I'm going ter 'ang messen, lad,' he told me, as though he'd done it a time or two already, and people had usually asked him questions like this beforehand.

'What for, mate?' He must have thought I was a nosy young bogger.

''Cause I want to, that's what for,' he said, clearing all the pots off the table and pulling it to the middle of the room. Then he stood on it to fasten the rope to the light-fitting. The table creaked and didn't look very safe, but it did him for what he wanted.

'It wain't hold up, mate,' I said to him, thinking how much better it was being here than sitting in the pictures and seeing the Jungle Jim serial.

But he got nettled now and turned on me. 'Mind yer own business.'

I thought he was going to tell me to scram but he didn't. He made ever such a fancy knot with that rope, as though he'd been a sailor or summat, and as he tied it he was whistling a fancy tune to himself. Then he got down from the table and pushed it back to the wall, and put a chair in its place. He wasn't looking black at all, nowhere near as black, as anybody in our family when they're feeling fed-up. If ever he'd looked only half as black as our dad looked twice a week he'd have hanged himself years ago, I couldn't help thinking. But he was making a good job of that rope all right, as though he'd thought about it a lot anyway, and as though it was going to be the last thing he'd ever do. But I knew something he didn't know, because he wasn't standing where I was. I knew the rope wouldn't hold up, and I told him so, again.

'Shut yer gob,' he said, but quiet like, 'or I'll kick yer out.'

I didn't want to miss it, so I said nothing. He took his cap off and put it on the dresser, then he took his coat off, and his scarf, and spread them out on the sofa. I wasn't a bit frightened, like I might be now at sixteen, because it was interesting. And being only ten I'd never had a chance to see a bloke hang himself before.

We got pally, the two of us, before he slipped the rope around his neck.

'Shut the door,' he asked me, and I did as I was told. 'Ye're a good lad for your age,' he said to me while I sucked my thumb, and he felt in his pockets and pulled out all that was inside, throwing the handful of bits and bobs on the table: fag-packet and peppermints, a pawn-ticket, an old comb, and a few coppers. He picked out a penny and gave it to me, saying: 'Now listen ter me, young 'un, I'm going to 'ang messen, and when I'm swinging I want you to gi' this chair a bloody good kick and push it away. All right?'

I nodded.

He put the rope around his neck, and then took it off like it was a tie that didn't fit. 'What are yer going to do it for, mate?' I asked again.

'Because I'm fed-up,' he said, looking very unhappy. 'And because I want to. My missus left me, and I'm out o' work.'

I didn't want to argue, because the way he said it, I knew he couldn't do anything else except hang himself. Also there was a funny look in his face: even when he talked to me I swear he couldn't see me. It was different to the black looks my old man puts on, and I suppose that's why my old man would never hang himself, worse luck, because he never gets a look into his clock like this bloke had. My old man's look stares at you, so that you have to back down and fly out of the house: this bloke's look looked through you, so that you could face it and know it wouldn't do you any harm. So I saw now that dad would never hang himself because he could never get the right sort of look into his face, in spite of the fact that he'd been out of work often enough. Maybe mam would have to leave him first, and then he might do it;

but no—I shook my head there wasn't much chance of that even though he did lead her a dog's life.

'Yer wain't forget to kick that chair away?' he reminded me, and I swung my head to say I wouldn't. So my eyes were popping and I watched every move he made. He stood on the chair and put the rope around his neck so that it fitted this time, still whistling his fancy tune. I wanted to get a better goz at the knot, because my pal was in the scouts, and would ask to know how it was done, and if I told him later he'd let me know what happened at the pictures in the Jungle Jim serial, so's I could have my cake and eat it as well as mam says, tit for tat. But I thought I'd better not ask the bloke to tell me, and I stayed back in my corner. The last thing he did was take the wet, dirty butt-end from his lips and sling it into the empty firegrate, following it with his eyes to the black fireback where it landed—as if he was then going to mend a fault in the lighting like any electrician.

Suddenly his long legs wriggled and his feet tried to kick the chair, so I helped him as I'd promised I would and took a runner at it as if I was playing centre-forward for Notts Forest, and the chair went scooting back against the sofa, dragging his muffler to the floor as it tipped over. He swung for a bit, his arms chafing like he was a scarecrow flapping birds away and he made a noise in his throat as if he'd just took a dose of salts and was trying to make them stay down.

Then there was another sound, and I looked up and saw a big crack come in the ceiling, like you see on the pictures when an earthquake's happening, and the bulb began circling round and round as though it was a space ship. I was just beginning to get dizzy when, thank Christ, he fell down with such a horrible thump on the floor that I thought he'd broke every bone he'd got. He kicked around for a bit like a dog that's got colic bad. Then he lay still.

I didn't stay to look at him. 'I told him that rope wouldn't hold up,' I kept saying to myself as I went out of the house, tut-tutting because he hadn't done the job right, hands stuffed deep into my pockets and nearly crying at the balls-up he'd made of everything. I slammed his gate so hard with disappointment that it nearly dropped off its hinges.

Just as I was going back up the yard to get my tea at home, hoping the others had come back from the picture so's I wouldn't have anything to keep on being black about, a copper passed me and headed for the bloke's door. He was striding quickly with his head bent forward, and I knew that somebody had marked. They must have seen him buy the rope and then tipped off the cop. Or happen the old hen at the yard-end had finally caught on. Or perhaps he'd even told somebody himself, because I supposed that the bloke who'd strung himself up hadn't much known what he was doing, especially with the look I'd seen in his eyes. But that's how it is, I said to myself, as I followed the copper back to the bloke's house, poor bloke can't even hang himself these days.

When I got back the copper was slitting the rope from his neck with a pen-knife, then he gave him a drink of water, and the bloke opened his peepers. I didn't like the copper, because he'd got a couple of my mates sent to approved school for pinching lead piping from lavatories.

'What did you want to hang yourself for?' he asked the bloke, trying to make him sit up. He could hardly talk, and one of his hands was bleeding from where the light-bulb had smashed. I knew that rope wouldn't hold up, but he hadn't listened to me. I'll never hang myself anyway, but if I want to I'll make sure I do it from a tree or something like that, not a light fitting. 'Well, what did you do it for?'

'Because I wanted to,' the bloke croaked.

'You'll get five years for this,' the copper told him. I'd crept back into the house and was sucking my thumb in the same corner.

'That's what yo' think,' the bloke said, a normal frightened look in his eyes now. 'I only wanted to hang myself.'

'Well,' the copper said, taking out his book, 'it's against the law, you know.'

'Nay,' the bloke said, 'it can't be. It's my life, ain't it?'

'You might think so,' the copper said, 'but it ain't.'

He began to suck the blood from his hand. It was such a little scratch though that you couldn't see it. 'That's the first thing I knew,' he said.

'Well, I'm telling you,' the copper told him.

''Course, I didn't let on to the copper that I'd helped the bloke to hang himself. I wasn't born yesterday, nor the day before yesterday either.

'It's fine thing if a bloke can't take his own life,' the bloke said, seeing he was in for it.

'Well he can't, it ain't your life. And it's a crime to take your own life. It's killing yourself. It's suicide.'

The bloke looked hard, as if every one of the copper's words meant six-months cold. I felt sorry for him, and that's a fact, but if only he'd listened to what I'd said and not depended on that light-fitting. He should have done it from a tree, or something like that

He went up the yard with the copper like a peaceful lamb, and we all thought that that was the end of that.

But a couple of days later the news was flashed through to us—even before it got to the *Post* because a woman in our yard worked at the hospital of an evening dishing grub out and tidying up. I heard her spilling it to somebody at the yard-end. 'I'd never 'ave thought it. I thought he'd got that daft idea out of his head when they took him away. But no. Wonders'll never cease. Chucked 'issen from the hospital window when the copper who sat near his bed went off for a pee. Would you believe it? Dead? Not much 'e ain't.'

He'd heaved himself at the glass, and fallen like a stone on to the road. In one way I was sorry he'd done it, but in another I was glad, because he'd proved to the coppers and everybody whether it was his life or not all right. It was marvellous though, the way the brainless bastards had put him in a ward six floors up, which finished him off, proper, even better than a tree.

All of which will make me think twice about how black I sometimes feel. The black coal-bag locked inside you, and the back look it puts on your face, doesn't mean you're going to string yourself up or sling yourself under a double-decker or chuck yourself out of a window or cut your throat with a sardine-tin or put your head in the gas-oven or drop your rotten sack-bag of a body on to a railway line, because when you're feeling that black you can't even move from your chair. Anyhow, I know I'll never get so black as to hang myself, because hanging don't look very nice to me, and never will, the more I remember old what's his-name swinging from the light-fitting.

More than anything else, I'm glad now I didn't go to the pictures that Saturday afternoon when I was feeling black and ready to do myself in. Because you know, I shan't ever kill myself. Trust me. I'll stay alive half-barmy till I'm a hundred and five, and then go out screaming blue murder because I want to stay where I am.

New words

[*Note*:—(dial): dialect
(coll): colloquial]

bloke:	(coll) a man
to string oneself up:	(sl) to hang oneself
saccharine:	substitute for sugar
Sunday-joint maulers:	huge hands like large pieces of meat
scrunched:	(dial) bent
broody:	feeling bad-tempered
to go crackers:	(sl) go mad
to mash tea:	(dial) to make tea
clink:	(sl) prison
plugged:	(sl) stuck
summat:	(dial) something
bookie:	(coll) short for 'bookmaker'; man who takes bets of money on a horse race
to fib:	(coll) to tell a lie
to bash away:	(sl) to work hard
messen:	(dial) myself
bogger:	(dial) (a swear word)
bits and bobs:	(sl) small useless things of little value
goz:	(sl) look
Nott's Forest:	short for Nottingham Forest—a football team in England
to chafe:	move up and down
colic:	pains in the stomach
balls-up:	(sl) a mess
copper, cop:	(coll) policeman
to mark:	(sl) to inform the police

peepers:	(sl) eyes
approved school:	school for young criminals
to croak:	to speak with difficulty as when one has a bad cold
to let on:	(sl) to tell
to be in for it:	(sl) to be in trouble
six-months cold:	(sl) six months in prison
grub:	(coll) food
spill:	(sl) to tell
daft:	(coll) silly
'issen:	(dial) himself
to go off for a pee:	(sl) go to the lavatory
to do oneself in:	(sl) to kill oneself
barmy:	(sl) half mad
to scream blue murder:	(sl) to scream very loudly

Comprehension

1. Why was the little boy feeling miserable one Saturday afternoon? What is the expression the author uses to suggest the boy's feelings that afternoon? What was the great event he witnessed that day? Did he enjoy it? Why?

2. At which moments did the boy's family look thoroughly 'black'? How did the father behave when, for instance, he did not have a packet of cigarettes? What cheered him up one day when he was in one of his bad moods?

3. 'Black looks run in the family.' Why does the author say this? Does he think that other families also suffer from frequent fits of ill-temper? Is the behaviour of

the other families at such moments any different from that of the boy's family? How is it different?

4. Why did the father ask his son to go outside and get some fresh air that Saturday afternoon? Was the air outside the boy's house fresh? Why not? Can you describe the man who the little boy saw? Did the woman in the yard believe the man when he said that he was going to hang himself?

5. Did the man realise that the little boy was watching him make his preparations? Did he mind the boy's presence? How did he react when he was told that the rope would not 'hold up'? What was the boy's age then? How old is he when he tells the story?

6. Did the man and the boy become friends? What did the man want the boy to do in return for the penny he gave him? What was his reason for wanting to commit suicide? Did the boy think that the man's decision was justified?

7. Was the man tense while getting ready to hang himself or, was he relaxed? Why did the boy want to find out what kind of a knot the man had made? Can you describe what happened when the man finally performed his act?

8. How did the boy react when the hanging proved unsuccessful? Who do *you* think must have let the police know about the attempted suicide? Why didn't the boy like that particular policeman? The policeman says: 'You'll get five years for this.' What did he mean?

9. What was the man's argument in favour of his attempted suicide? What was the policeman's argument against it? Why didn't the boy confess his part in the incident? Does he feel sorry for the man? Why?

10 How did the man finally die? What stupid mistake did the police make which helped the man to succeed the second time? Would the boy ever perform a similar act? Why not?

Steps to Interpretation

1. Do you think that the boy was distinctly lucky to have witnessed a suicide attempt? Why do you think so? Do you think any other boy of the same age would also have enjoyed the spectacle? The boy was ten years old when the incident took place. What difference would it have made if he had been six years older?
2. What is your impression of the boy's father? What do you think of his relationship with his wife and son in this story? Do you think the family had no financial problems? Could this be the reason for their frequent attacks of depression?
3. Where is the boy's house located, in the countryside or in a congested industrial area in a large town? Is there any evidence to support your answer? One of the reasons why the man wants to end his life is that he is unemployed. Do you think the author is hinting at the evil consequences of economic problems like unemployment in cities? Does a man have the right to take his own life even if society does not allow it?
4. What kind of a person is the little boy in the story? (For instance compare him with Schatz who appears in 'A Day's Wait'.)

   At times he is still a baby (He is ten years old but still sucks his thumb) but at other moments he behaves as a thoroughly mature person. Can you indicate the points in the story when he seems mature? Like the boy in the story, would *you* have felt disappointed too if the person committing suicide in your presence failed in his attempt?
5. You notice that Sillitoe freely uses colloquial language mixed with slang and dialect words. How does the language reflect the character of the boy, the man and the policeman? Do you think Sillitoe would have achieved the same effect if he had used 'proper' English unmixed with slang and colloquialisms?